INVERCLYDE LIBRARIES

	PORT GLASGOW	

This book is to be returned on or before the last date above. It may be borrowed for a further period if not in demand.

For enquiries and renewals Tel: (01475) 712323
www.inverclyde.gov.uk/libraries

QUEEN ELIZABETH II

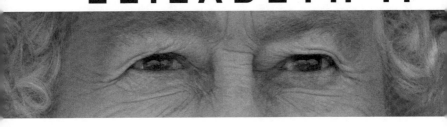

POCKET
GIANTS

VICTORIA ARBITER

Cover image © PA Photos

First published 2016

The History Press
The Mill, Brimscombe Port
Stroud, Gloucestershire, GL5 2QG
www.thehistorypress.co.uk

British Library Cataloguing in Publication Data.
A catalogue record for this book is available from the British Library.

ISBN 978 0 7509 6616 0

Typesetting and origination by The History Press
Printed and bound in Malta, by Melita Press.

Contents

Acknowledgements

Thank you to Rosemary Arbiter, Tony Burton, Marlene Koenig and William Rycroft for your ever-present brilliance. My thanks to Tony Morris for delivering deadlines, critiques and notes in such a positive and encouraging fashion. It's been a delight. Profound gratitude to my father, Dickie Arbiter, for parking my 6-year-old self atop the LBC News van for Trooping the Colour … where it all began. And finally, my thanks to Ryan and Raff Brown, with whom all things really are possible.

Introduction

The New Elizabethan Era

I have to be seen to be believed.

Elizabeth II, tour to New Zealand,
March 1970[1]

Descending the stairs of the royal plane at London Airport on 7 February 1952, the former Princess Elizabeth took her first steps on British soil as queen. She was 25. Only days earlier, her parents, King George VI and Queen Elizabeth, along with her sister, Princess Margaret, had joined a crowd 3000-strong to bid farewell to their eldest daughter and her husband, the Duke of Edinburgh, as they pepared to depart for a five-month tour of Australia and New Zealand. Due to her father's declining health, Elizabeth had already represented him at a number of public engagements, and had only recently returned from a tour to Canada on his behalf, but in early 1952, as the king's condition showed signs of improvement, it was decided that he was well enough for the young princess to embark on a tour that would see her travel 30,000 miles across four continents.

After sharing a private goodbye on board the aircraft, the royal family returned to the tarmac. With a final wave from the king, the door closed and the plane began its taxi. It was the last time Elizabeth saw her father. Six days later, on 6 February, during the couple's stay at Treetops Hotel in Kenya, the first stop on the tour, a *Reuters* press flash alerted the accompanying media that the king had died in his sleep at Sandringham early that morning. He was 56.

At 2.45 p.m. local time, once the princess' private secretary, Martin Charteris, had confirmed the news, Prince Philip informed Elizabeth of her father's death. Following a nineteen-hour flight, the royal plane landed back at London Airport where a small group of Elizabeth's ministers, led by her uncle, the Duke of Gloucester, and Prime Minister Winston Churchill, waited to greet her. The royal couple drove to Clarence House in a car bearing the Sovereign's Arms, and the next day, 8 February 1952, the accession of Her Majesty Queen Elizabeth II was proclaimed.

At the time of her birth Princess Elizabeth was never expected to ascend the throne. Were it not for the 1936 abdication of her uncle, Edward VIII, the monarchy as it exists today would be very different indeed. Edward was never crowned and his reign lasted a mere 325 days. Had he fulfilled his kingly duties he would have been required to marry and provide an heir and a spare, but his infatuation with twice-divorced American socialite, Wallis Simpson, and subsequent abdication led to an unprecedented and dramatic shift within the House of Windsor. As his brother's successor, King George VI renewed the general populace's faith in the centuries-old institution, which had been badly shaken as a result of Edward's actions. In turn he proved himself to be far better suited to the role of kingship than his elder brother. Re-establishing a sense of national unity, he led his country through the war years, and his popularity in life gave way to public affection for Elizabeth upon his death.

Most Britons alive today have never known any other sovereign, and with more than sixty years as head of the world's most famous family, it is hard for many to imagine a Britain in which Elizabeth II is not the head of state. She is the nation's fortieth monarch and only the sixth queen since William the Conqueror took the crown more than a thousand years ago. As Britain's longest reigning monarch – having surpassed Queen Victoria's record on 9 September 2015 – she is also the country's longest-lived monarch, as well as the world's oldest-serving sovereign. In addition to the UK, she is head of state to fifteen other nations known as the Realms and serves as the symbolic leader of the fifty-three-member Commonwealth of Nations. Unlike her mother, she has never been viewed as the nation's favourite 'twinkly eyed granny'.

Elizabeth's reign has granted the country stability and continuity; she has presided over many of the greatest socio-economic changes of the twentieth century. Her rule has spanned twelve British prime ministers, twelve US presidents and seven popes. At the request of her government she has had dealings with countless global leaders and political heroes and villains including presidents Gorbachev, Eisenhower and Mugabe, South African leader Nelson Mandela, Indian prime minister Indira Gandhi, Romanian dictator Nicolae Ceausescu and IRA commander Martin McGuiness. Over the course of the twentieth century she has signed documents giving independence to hundreds of millions of citizens across the world, and yet it is on the domestic front that she has overseen many of the monarchy's most significant reforms. During her sovereignty the royal family has overhauled its personal finances, resulting in a 1992 agreement for the queen to start paying income tax. In 2011, Elizabeth approved changes to the laws to succession, allowing first-born daughters to take precedence over younger-born brothers, as well as permitting future heirs to marry Roman Catholics (even if they themselves may not convert to Catholicism). These sweeping modifications, long overdue in the eyes of many critics, put an end to laws dating back over 300 years. In 2013, before a global press, Elizabeth signed the historic Commonwealth Charter – a single document unanimously approved by members of the Commonwealth – setting out the core values of the organisation and demanding equality for all.

In 1958 the queen abolished the presentation of the debutantes, which had historically marked the start to the social season. Later she made the 'walkabout' the norm, embraced the world of social media and, in 1993, agreed to open Buckingham Palace to the paying public for a few months of the year. Today the monarchy, although considered aloof and out of touch by some observers, has its own website and Facebook account, not to mention a presence on YouTube, Flickr and Instagram. The announcement of Prince George's birth in July 2013 was placed on an easel in the forecourt of Buckingham Palace, as had been the tradition for previous royal babies … but not before the news was beamed around the world via Twitter. The queen is well aware that in order to remain relevant in the twenty-first century, modern communication has to be incorporated.

Whether allowing herself to be filmed at Buckingham Palace with James Bond and corgis in tow for the opening ceremony of the London 2012 Olympics, or solidifying the peace process in Northern Ireland by sharing a symbolic handshake with the leaders of Sinn Féin, the queen has remained above party politics while retaining her place in the public's affection. The chances of the world witnessing another reign as long and eventful as hers are slim. Her place in history is secure. Though many Britons are reluctant to acknowledge the inevitable day when the mantle of sovereignty will pass to her eldest son, Charles, the Prince of Wales, the queen will leave a neatly packaged monarchy for which many archaic laws have been changed, hands of friendship have been extended and popularity stands at an all-time high.

It has been more than sixty years since the queen took her Coronation Oath in Westminster Abbey. A devoutly religious woman, she solemnly swore to 'govern her people, cause Law and Justice in mercy to be executed, and maintain the Laws of God and the true profession of the Gospel', before the Archbishop of Canterbury, Geoffrey Fisher, anointed her with oil and placed St Edward's Crown upon her head. In commemoration of her Diamond Jubilee in 2012, speaking before both Houses of Parliament in Westminster Hall, she rededicated herself to her role, declaring:

> We are reminded here of our past, of the continuity of our national story and the virtues of resilience, ingenuity and tolerance which created it. I have been privileged to witness some of that history and, with the support of my family, rededicate myself to the

> service of our great country and its people now and
> in the years to come.[2]

Her words offered a clear indication that she has no
intention of stepping aside, and echoed the commitment
she made in a radio address on her 21st birthday in 1947.
In the broadcast, made to the Commonwealth during a
tour to Southern Africa with her parents, she said, 'I declare
before you all that my whole life, whether it be long or
short, shall be devoted to your service and the service of
our great imperial family to which we all belong.'[3]

The world today is far less deferential than when
Elizabeth ascended the throne, but through consistency,
commitment and devotion to duty, she has managed to
win over many ardent Republicans who have declared her
to be 'untouchable'. Even as Scottish nationalists looked to
the 2014 referendum on independence, they vowed to keep
the queen as head of state regardless of the vote's outcome.

In terms of her place in pop culture, Elizabeth II is
one of the most instantly recognisable women in the
world and has inspired countless storytellers and artists
during her six decades on the British throne. There are
books lending insight into every facet of her life, from
her wardrobe, palaces and jewels to the contents of her
handbag. Children's offerings include *Paddington at the
Palace* and the slightly less reverent *The Queen's Knickers*,
and classic literary figures such as Christopher Robin and
Alice have visited Buckingham Palace in their fictional
escapades. Her likeness even appeared on the silver screen
alongside Leslie Nielson in the hit comedy *The Naked Gun*.

Dame Helen Mirren has portrayed her so successfully – both on stage and screen – that Prince William cheekily referred to her as 'Granny' when he presented Mirren with the BAFTA Fellowship in 2013. There are Warhol portraits and *Spitting Image* puppets. Even an album cover by legendary punk band The Sex Pistols bears her image. She is featured on stamps, money, china, biscuit tins, bobbleheads and tea towels the world over, but as enticing as her global fame may seem, it has come at a significant personal cost, beginning with the death of her father.

Her formal title is: Her Majesty Elizabeth the Second, by the Grace of God of the United Kingdom of Great Britain and Northern Ireland, and of Her other Realms and Territories Queen, Head of the Commonwealth, Defender of the Faith, but historians will remember her as the monarch, wife, mother, grandmother and great-grandmother who presided over a second Elizabethan Age – a giant among British royals.

A Princess is Born

She has an authority and reflectiveness astonishing in an infant.

Winston Churchill, 1928[4]

Their Royal Highnesses the Duke and Duchess of York – Prince Albert and his wife, Elizabeth Bowes-Lyon – welcomed their first child, a daughter, at 2.40 a.m. on 21 April 1926. Princess Elizabeth Alexandra Mary of York was born by caesarean section at No. 17 Bruton Street, Mayfair, London, the home of her maternal grandparents. In those days it was customary for the home secretary to attend and verify a royal birth, so, although he was not in the actual delivery room, Sir William Joynson Hicks was present in the house. It was, perhaps, a somewhat inauspicious start given Elizabeth is the only monarch ever to have been born at a residential address with a street number, but upon her birth she assumed her place as third in line to the throne. Her grandfather, King George V, was plagued by a multitude of health issues, but he retained his title for a further ten years after her birth, during which time his eldest son and successor Edward, the Prince of Wales, was expected to marry and father children of his own. It was believed highly unlikely Elizabeth would ever be crowned.

In May 1926 the Anglican Archbishop of York, Cosmo Lang, christened the new princess in the private chapel at Buckingham Palace. She was named after her mother, the youngest daughter of Scottish aristocrat Claude Bowes-Lyon, 14th Earl of Strathmore and Kinghorne. Her middle names were given in tribute to her paternal great-grandmother, Queen Alexandra, who had died six months earlier, and her paternal grandmother, Queen Mary. As a small child she had difficulty pronouncing Elizabeth and so she referred to herself as 'Lilibet', a name her close family still calls her today.

The new family divided its time between a London townhouse at 145 Piccadilly and White Lodge in Richmond Park. Unburdened by the stresses imposed on his older brother as Heir Apparent, Albert was an attentive, hands-on father and he relished the time at home with his wife and new daughter. In a letter to his mother, Queen Mary, he wrote, 'You don't know what a tremendous joy it is to Elizabeth and me to have our little girl.'[5] Much like modern royal babies, the princess' birth generated keen public interest. Silent black-and-white news bulletins of the day presented film footage of 'Little Princess "Betty" accompanied by her nurse out for an afternoon drive in the park'. When Elizabeth was just 9 months old her parents embarked on a six-month tour to Australia and New Zealand, leaving their baby in the care of the Countess of Strathmore at her home in Hertfordshire. Her nanny, Clara Knight (affectionately known as Alah), oversaw her daily routine and sent the queen regular updates detailing her young charge's progress. One such letter, dated 8 March 1927, included a reassuring photograph of a smiling Elizabeth stating, 'If Mummy looks into my wide open mouth with a little magnifying glass she will see my two teeth.'[6]

Four years later, on 21 August 1930, Elizabeth's only sibling, Princess Margaret Rose of York, was born at Glamis

Castle in Scotland, the ancestral home of her mother. Now a family of four, the tight-knit Yorks maintained a happy household, and the duke and duchess were content to dispense with their nanny in order to oversee bathtime and read bedtime stories themselves. When Elizabeth was 6, they made Royal Lodge in the grounds of Windsor Great Park their country home and settled there under the watchful eye of Alah who, accompanied by Elizabeth's nursemaid Margaret (Bobo) MacDonald, conducted a strict regimen. The girls were educated privately at home. In 1933 Scottish governess, Marion Crawford (Crawfie), joined the royal household and the girls' lessons in history, literature, languages, mathematics, geography, art, dance and music began in earnest. Crawfie retired in 1948, shortly after a 21-year-old Elizabeth married the 26-year-old Duke of Edinburgh. The royal governess herself had wed just two months prior to Elizabeth, having postponed marital life for fear of being seen to abandon the king and queen. Bobo was to serve her mistress for sixty-seven years.

Elizabeth's was a contented childhood, albeit one that was somewhat isolating given the nature of her position. Often craving the company of children her own age, she developed a passion for dogs and horses. It was an unpretentious life in which manners and deference were prime ingredients, and by the age of 3 she had already mastered the art of the perfect curtsey. A kind and unspoilt little girl, she was utterly devoted to her parents, as they were to her. Home movies projected during the Buckingham Palace Royal Childhood Exhibition in 2014 reveal joyful footage of the princesses singing, dancing, gardening and riding. Elizabeth's father lovingly referred to her as his pride and Margaret his joy. But everything was to change on 11 December 1936, when Edward VIII announced his decision to renounce the throne in order to marry Mrs Simpson. The day before the abdication Albert went to London to see his mother, Queen Mary, and later wrote in his diary, 'When I told her what had happened [the news of his brother's impending abdication], I broke down and sobbed like a child.'[7] With a heavy heart, Albert reluctantly assumed the burden of sovereignty. He chose the regnal name George in an effort to boost public confidence in the monarchy and promote continuity. On 12 May 1937, the two princesses attended the coronation of their father, King George VI, and his queen at Westminster Abbey. Princess Elizabeth was the first female heir presumptive to witness the crowning of her parents.

The family moved into Buckingham Palace and Elizabeth began her studies in constitutional history and law under the guidance of Henry Marten, vice-provost of Eton College. She was instructed in religion by the Archbishop of Canterbury and mastered French with the help of a slew of native-speaking governesses. She continued to ride and became an accomplished swimmer. In June 1939, aged 13, she won the Children's Challenge Shield at London's Bath Club. A company of Girl Guides was brought in to provide Elizabeth with the companionship of children her own age. Thus was born the 1st Buckingham Palace Company, leading her later to become a Sea Ranger.

In May and June of 1939 the king and queen toured Canada – George being the first reigning monarch to do so. Elizabeth's father, believing her too young to undertake public engagements, insisted that she remain at home. When the Second World War was declared in September, it was George, a serving naval officer during the First World War, who informed his people, 'For the second time in the lives of most of us, we are at war.'[8] Elizabeth and Margaret were in residence at Birkhall in Scotland with their parents. The king and queen returned to London immediately, but the girls stayed in Scotland with Alah and Crawfie until Christmas, when they joined the rest of the royal family at Sandringham. Every effort was made to keep life as 'normal' as possible. When senior British politician Lord Hailsham suggested that the princesses be evacuated to the relative safety of Canada, their mother famously responded, 'The children could not go without me, I could not possibly leave the king, and the king would never go.'[9] So the girls were installed at Windsor Castle for the duration of the war. They sheltered in the dungeons during air raids. They joined a local Girl Guide group where they spent time with evacuees and it was from Windsor, on 13 October 1940, that a 14-year-old Princess Elizabeth delivered her first radio address. Speaking on *Children's Hour* she hoped to provide calm reassurance to the many children across the Commonwealth who had been displaced due to the war:

> We are trying to do all we can to help our gallant sailors, soldiers and airmen, and we are trying, too, to bear our share of the danger and sadness of war. We know, every one of us, that in the end all will be well

> … when peace comes, remember it will be for us, the children of today to make the world of tomorrow a better and happier place.[10]

In 1942 Princess Elizabeth was appointed colonel-in-chief of the Grenadier Guards, and on her 16th birthday she carried out her first joint public engagement, inspecting the troops at Windsor Castle. A year later she fulfilled her first solo public engagement, spending the day with a Grenadier Guards' tank battalion. Over the following months her official duties steadily increased. She accompanied her parents on a number of occasions as they made morale-boosting visits to bomb sites and munitions factories. She became president of the Queen Elizabeth Hospital for Children in Hackney, East London, and, in 1944, just shy of her 18th birthday, she was named one of four counsellors of state, thereby enabling her to act on her father's behalf in the event of his absence. A couple of months later, as her father travelled to Italy to inspect his troops, she executed some of the duties of the head of state for the first time. The princess embarked on her first official tour of Scotland with her parents in September 1944, and in July 1945 she took her first flight when she accompanied the king and queen on a two-day visit to Northern Ireland.

As hostilities raged on, Elizabeth was keen to make a more significant contribution to the war effort by joining one of the women's services. Her case was raised with the minister of labour, but it was decided that Elizabeth should not be allowed to enlist on the grounds of personal safety. She was not prepared to give up and campaigned persistently for permission to register. In early 1945 her father conceded and she joined the Women's Auxiliary Territorial Service (ATS), volunteering as a driver and mechanic. Learning to change tyres, fix engines and drive motor vehicles of all shapes and sizes, she toiled under the bonnet of a car by day and slept in the castle by night. Her service may have only lasted a few months, but it provided her invaluable insight into a world far beyond palace walls and, within five months, she was promoted to the rank of junior commander.

In order to graduate from training, every ATS member was required to drive a heavy vehicle from camp into London. Citing her safety once again, ministers decided that Elizabeth should not be permitted to complete the exam. They had underestimated her tenacity. Despite their protestations, Elizabeth defiantly drove her lumbering, camouflaged lorry through heavy traffic from the Camberley army depot to London. After successfully navigating Piccadilly Circus, she passed through the gates of Buckingham Palace. She had driven the entire route alone, but more importantly for the ministers present, she had done so without suffering or inflicting personal injury. Attending the 70th anniversary commemorations of D-Day in France in June 2014, the queen was the last remaining head of state present to have served in uniform during the Second World War, as had her consort, Prince Philip.

The 8 May 1945 marked VE Day. Celebrations erupted across the globe. In London, crowds amassed along The Mall to Buckingham Palace. The king and queen appeared on the balcony alongside their daughters – Elizabeth wearing her ATS uniform – and Prime Minister Winston Churchill. In a rare recording for the BBC in 1985, Elizabeth recalled, 'We asked my parents if we could go out and see for ourselves. I remember we were terrified of being recognised … I remember lines of unknown people linking arms and walking down Whitehall, all of us swept along on a tide of happiness and relief.'[11] She concluded, 'It was one of the most memorable nights of my life.' Never again would the queen be able to fraternise with the public in such a fashion.

Elizabeth embarked on her first overseas tour on 31 January 1947, joining her parents and sister on a trip to the Union of South Africa and Rhodesia. It was the first international royal visit since the outbreak of war in 1939, and the first time a reigning British monarch had set foot on South African soil. As Britain endured its worst winter of the century, HMS *Vanguard* set sail from Portsmouth, arriving in the warmer climes of Cape Town on 17 February. It was from there that Elizabeth later delivered her now infamous 21st birthday radio address. She would not visit South Africa again until 1995, following the country's first democratic elections and subsequent end to apartheid.

Over the course of three months the family travelled to forty-two different locations across two countries before departing for home on 24 April. There were guard inspections, parades, garden parties and balls, but never was there a mention of the announcement that was to be made upon the family's return to London – one that would change the course of Elizabeth's life.

A Royal Romance

He [Philip] has quite simply been my strength and stay all these years, and I owe him a debt greater than he would ever claim.

Elizabeth II, Golden Wedding
Anniversary speech, 1997[12]

Princess Elizabeth first met Prince Philip of Greece and Denmark, her third cousin through Queen Victoria, at the age of 8. She was serving as a bridesmaid at the wedding of her uncle, the Duke of Kent, to Princess Marina at Westminster Abbey. Philip, a first cousin of Marina, was a guest at the service. Five years later, following a visit to the Royal Naval College Dartmouth with her parents and sister in July 1939, Elizabeth was smitten. Philip, by then an 18-year-old blonde-haired, blue-eyed mid-shipman, was charged with keeping the king's daughters entertained while their parents toured the grounds. The king himself had been a cadet at the college in the days before the Great War and the visit offered the girls a glimpse into their father's past. It also allowed Lord Louis Mountbatten, 'Uncle Dickie', a chance to dabble in a little matchmaking between his nephew and the king's eldest daughter.

Philip had been at Dartmouth for only a year, but had already won the King's Dirk for best all-rounder, and the Eardley-Howard-Crockett prize for the best cadet. In 1940, with war underway, he joined HMS *Ramillies* in Colombo and spent six months serving in the Indian Ocean. As the war progressed, so too did Philip's naval career. He was mentioned in despatches for his role in the night action off Cape Matapan, the southernmost point of mainland

Greece, while posted aboard HMS *Valiant* in March 1941 and, by the age of 21, had already been promoted to the role of first lieutenant aboard HMS *Wallace*.

Throughout his time at sea Elizabeth kept his photograph on her dressing table, and the couple's courtship flourished through letters. When she turned 16, the princess appointed her first lady-in-waiting to assist with her correspondence. Her parents noted that almost all of it was either to or from Philip.

The princesses' annual Christmas pantomimes at Windsor Castle allowed the young suitors an opportunity to reunite. Philip attended their 1943 production of *Aladdin*, and as he watched the scenes unfold from his seat in the front row, Crawfie noted, 'I have never known Lilibet more animated. There was a sparkle about her none of us had ever seen before.'[13]

Once war ended, Elizabeth and Philip were seen together in an official capacity far more frequently and, in 1946, Philip asked the king for his daughter's hand in marriage. Though he liked Philip well enough, the proposal was not looked upon favourably; George feared Elizabeth was still too young to marry. There was also concern over Philip's boisterous personality and rumoured eye for the ladies, but it was clear that he made Elizabeth very happy. George agreed to give his consent, but only on the condition that the news would not be made public until after Elizabeth's 21st birthday, by which time the family would have returned from its official visit to South Africa. Over the ensuing months Philip renounced his Greek and Danish royal titles, as well as his allegiance to the Greek Crown. The Greek Orthodox Church and Church of England were technically in communion, but he chose to be formally received into the Anglican Church by the Archbishop of Canterbury. He became a naturalised British citizen and adopted the surname Mountbatten from his maternal grandparents.

The couple's engagement was finally announced just before midnight on 9 July 1947, and four months later, on 20 November, they were married at Westminster Abbey. The day prior to the wedding, the king granted Philip the style 'His Royal Highness', and on the morning of the ceremony he bestowed Philip with the titles Duke of Edinburgh, Earl of Merioneth and Baron of Greenwich. Even though he had given up his Greek royal titles upon his British naturalisation, the press continued to refer to the newly conferred duke as Prince Philip. Ten years later, in 1957, the title became official when the queen created him a prince of the United Kingdom and Northern Ireland.

The betrothal was not entirely without controversy. Philip was foreign born and had no independent financial standing. His surviving sisters, all married to German noblemen, were not invited to the wedding as a mark of post-war sensitivity. The newly titled Duke of Windsor, formerly King Edward VIII, was living in exile in France and was also denied an invitation. But as the grey morning dawned, thousands of spectators flocked towards the Mall as others lined Whitehall, eager to witness the procession. Crowds gathered around loud speakers to hear the royal couple declare their vows and outside the abbey spontaneous cheers erupted as invitees, many of whom included members of Europe's rapidly disappearing royal families, arrived to take their seats.

With post-war austerity measures still in place, Elizabeth was required to collect ration coupons to purchase the material necessary to make her wedding dress. Norman Hartnell designed her delicate silk tulle veil and ivory silk gown with a 15ft train. The dress was embroidered with crystals and 10,000 pearls brought in from America.

The timing of the occasion was meticulous. Elizabeth and her father departed Buckingham Palace for Westminster Abbey in the Irish State Coach at 11.16 a.m. Before a congregation of 2,000, the Archbishop of Canterbury officiated the ceremony, which began at 11.30 a.m. The BBC recorded the occasion to broadcast to a global audience numbering 200 million. Unlike subsequent royal brides – Lady Diana Spencer and Catherine Middleton – Elizabeth's vows included the old-fashioned promise to 'obey'.

Following the service a wedding breakfast was held at Buckingham Palace, after which the newlyweds departed for their honeymoon at Broadlands in Hampshire, the home of Lord Mountbatten, before a sojourn at Birkhall on the Balmoral Estate. Not wishing to be separated from her beloved companion, Elizabeth's corgi Susan (which had been a gift for her 18th birthday), accompanied the couple. It was a day of much needed celebration. The pomp, pageantry and tempered grandeur served to remind Britons of happier, less austere, times and allowed for a sense of optimism and hope for the future.

Elizabeth and Philip leased Windlesham Moor, a country house near Windsor Castle, and three months later the princess was pregnant with the couple's first child. At 9.14 p.m. on 14 November 1948, six days before his parents' first wedding anniversary, Prince Charles Philip Arthur George was born at Buckingham Palace. Today fathers regularly remain in the delivery room for the birth of their child, but as Elizabeth was in the throes of labour, Prince Philip elected to take part in a game of squash on the Buckingham Palace court.

In October 1948, one month before Charles' birth, George VI issued letters patent granting any children born to Elizabeth and Philip the style of Royal Highness, along with the titular dignity of prince or princess prefixed to their Christian names, thereby ensuring Charles was born a royal prince. He also dispensed with a particularly archaic royal custom by decreeing that the Home Secretary need no longer be present for the baby's arrival, consigning lingering fears over illegitimate baby smuggling to the seventeenth century.

After Charles' christening – held in the Music Room at Buckingham Palace due to the private chapel having been destroyed during the war – Elizabeth wrote to a friend, 'Don't you think he is quite adorable? I still can't believe he is really mine.'[14] In 1949 the family took up residence at Clarence House and in June, due to the king's prolonged illness, Elizabeth represented her father at Trooping the Colour, the sovereign's official birthday parade, for the first time. Philip, meanwhile, was granted permission to resume active duty later that year. Between Christmas and the summer of 1951 he and Elizabeth lived intermittently in Malta, where Philip was stationed as a Royal Naval officer. He had been assigned his own command aboard HMS *Magpie*, and the couple's days living in the former Crown Colony offered a carefree and happy time together amidst the relative privacy of the Mediterranean isle. Prince Charles remained at home in the care of his nanny and grandparents while, for a short time, his mother experienced a life as normal as one in her position could hope for.

Elizabeth returned to London in 1950 to assume more of her father's responsibilities. Shortly thereafter, on 15 August, her only daughter, Princess Anne Elizabeth Alice Louise, was born at Clarence House. Though outwardly the royal family appeared relaxed, the punishing schedule of meetings and visits often led to weeks, even months, apart for parents and children. Burdened by constitutional obligations, Elizabeth was only able to spend half an hour with her children before her day's engagements. In the evening she returned home for a brief period of playtime before bathing them and putting them to bed. Charles has often spoken of his unhappy childhood, assuaged only by the nurturing relationship he shared with his nanny, Mabel Anderson, who filled the void left by his duty-bound mother. At the age of 8 he was enrolled at Hill House, an exclusive private school in West London. It was a progressive move on the part of his parents, and signalled the first time an heir apparent had been educated alongside regular children, albeit those of the fee-paying upper classes. For the queen, who as a child had largely been deprived of companions her own age, it was seen as an effort to provide Charles with as 'normal' a life as possible, but his ongoing school years proved to be among the most challenging of his life.

In September 1951, George VI's left lung was removed. He was a heavy smoker and had been diagnosed with cancer. In order to allow him time to convalesce, it was decided that Elizabeth and Philip should travel in his place on a state visit to Canada and the United States. So it was on 7 October 1951, that the British heir to the throne flew across the Atlantic for the first time, a journey that took sixteen-and-a-quarter hours. The trip proved a great success and, upon their return, Elizabeth and Philip were once again asked to represent the king and queen on another state visit, this time to Australia and New Zealand. In the months before their scheduled departure, on 31 January 1952, the family had much to celebrate: they gathered for a service of Thanksgiving in recognition of the king's recovery; November saw Prince Charles' third birthday, and, on 14 December, George turned 56. The night before Elizabeth and Philip's flight to Kenya – the first stop on their journey south – they joined the king, queen and Princess Margaret at the Drury Lane Theatre in London's West End for a production of *South Pacific*. Little did Elizabeth know, as she took in the spectacle from her seat in the royal box, that it would be their last night together.

A Crowning Moment

I want to ask you all, whatever your religion may be, to pray for me. To pray that Christ may give me wisdom and strength to carry out the solemn promises I shall be making and that I may faithfully serve him and you all the days of my life.

Elizabeth II, Christmas address to the
Commonwealth, 1952[15]

non-existent, and it wasn't until a local journalist asked Martin Charteris, the queen's private secretary, if reports of the king's death were true, that the royal party learned of George VI's passing. Elizabeth was among the last to be informed. Once the news was confirmed, preparations for the onward journey were abandoned and attention turned to matters of state. Charteris was charged with opening and preparing the sealed accession documents, which had been taken on tour as a precaution given the ongoing nature of the king's illness. Prince Albert had chosen to become King George VI as opposed to King Albert but when posed with the question of what regnal name she would choose, Elizabeth famously replied, 'My own name of course – what else?'[16] Mourning clothes were transported from Mombasa; telegrams were drafted and sent to her Kenyan hosts as well as those expecting her in Australia and New Zealand, and letters were penned to her mother and sister. When it came time to leave, Elizabeth asked that no pictures be taken. Witnessing her historic departure first-hand, reporters honoured her request.

On the evening of 7 February, Elizabeth arrived home to a nation in mourning. For many Britons her father had restored their faith in the monarchy and the shock over his death was widespread. The next morning, dressed in black, Elizabeth read her Declaration of Sovereignty before the assembled Accession Council at St James's Palace. The queen's proclamation rang out across London as Elizabeth and Philip made the solemn journey to Sandringham. The king's coffin was to rest in St Mary Magdalene church on the family estate until it was transported to London on 11 February for his lying in state at Westminster Hall. Mourners queued for more than four hours to pay their respects before his funeral at St George's Chapel, Windsor on 15 February. Queen Mary had already buried two sons. The loss of her third left her too weak to attend his funeral in person and so she watched the procession unfold from her home at Marlborough House. King George was interred in the Royal Vault until 1969, when his remains were moved to the King George VI Memorial Chapel at St George's Chapel. In 2002, fifty years after his death, his wife, Queen Elizabeth The Queen Mother passed away at the age of a 101. She was laid to rest beside him, along with the ashes of their youngest daughter, Princess Margaret, who had died only weeks earlier at the age of 71.

Contending with grief and the enormity of their new position, Elizabeth and Philip moved into Buckingham Palace while the Queen Mother and Princess Margaret took up residence at Clarence House. A former equerry to the king, Group-Captain Peter Townsend, who had travelled with the family on their tour to South Africa five years earlier, was appointed Comptroller of the Queen Mother's Household – an appointment that would later lead to scandal.

At the time of her accession it was widely believed that Elizabeth might be the last reigning Windsor monarch. Customarily women take their husband's name upon marriage, so there was the potential for a new house – the House of Mountbatten. In 1917 the queen's grandfather, King George V, issued a royal proclamation setting aside the German-sounding family name of Saxe-

Coburg and Gotha, thereby establishing the House of Windsor. His widow, Queen Mary, along with Prime Minister Winston Churchill, clearly stated their desire for Elizabeth to retain her house. On 9 April 1952 she formally announced that the House of Windsor would continue, leading to yet another sacrifice on Philip's part. He subsequently lamented, 'I am the only man in the country not allowed to give his name to his own children.'[17] In 1960, long after Queen Mary's death and Churchill's resignation, the queen declared that any male-line descendants who did not carry royal titles should bear the name Mountbatten-Windsor.

Elizabeth's coronation was sixteen months in the planning. Allowing for an appropriate period of mourning and giving organisers the requisite time to prepare, the Coronation Council, under the guidance of Prince Philip, declared in June 1952 that the coronation would take place one year later, on 2 June 1953. Once again, Norman Hartnell was tasked with creating a gown for Elizabeth. The white silk dress bore embroidered floral emblems of Commonwealth countries as well as the Tudor rose of England, the Scottish thistle, Welsh leek and Irish shamrock. On the gown's left side, where Elizabeth's hand would rest for much of the day, there was an embroidered four-leaf clover. Elizabeth rehearsed the ceremony with her maids of honour in the ballroom at Buckingham Palace. Sheets were fastened together to replicate the 60ft coronation train, and she wore the Imperial State Crown as she went about her daily affairs in an effort to get accustomed to its feel and weight.

Born during the reign of Queen Victoria, Queen Mary had lived to see six monarchs but, aware of her own advancing years, she amended her will upon her son's death to ensure that all her worldly possessions would be left to Elizabeth. Believing that mourning for an ex-queen consort should not impede the crowning of a new sovereign, she also stated that, should she die before June, the coronation should proceed as planned. On 24 March 1953, ten weeks before the ceremony, Queen Mary succumbed to lung cancer at the age of 85. Just over a year after saying goodbye to her father, Queen Elizabeth bid farewell to her grandmother.

By 1953 Group-Captain Townsend, still in the employ of the Queen Mother, was a newly divorced father of two sons when he proposed to 22-year-old Princess Margaret. Though he was sixteen years her senior, she accepted and informed the queen of her wish to marry. Due to the Royal Marriages Act of 1772 – considered by some to be outdated legislation left over from the days of George III – members of the royal family under the age of 25 in the line of succession required permission from the reigning sovereign if they wished to marry. Failure to seek approval would result in the surrendering of all royal rights and financial benefits from the Civil List. Senior politicians opposed the prospect of the union between Townsend and Margaret; the Church of England did not permit remarriage after divorce and Churchill warned Elizabeth that the Dominion prime ministers were overwhelmingly against the marriage. Elizabeth recognised her sister's happiness but, in her role as head of the Church of

England, she could not be seen to condone such an engagement. With Queen Mary's recent death, her own approaching coronation and plans to embark on a six-month tour of the Commonwealth underway, Elizabeth asked the couple to wait a year, hoping the romance might wane. Her private secretary recommended that she post Townsend abroad, but she refused and transferred him to her own household. The controversy waged on in the press for another two years and it became ever more apparent that the only way the marriage could go ahead was if Margaret renounced her right to the throne. Instead, it was Townsend whom she renounced. On 31 October 1955, two months after her 25th birthday, Margaret issued a statement: 'I would like it to be known that I have decided not to marry Group-Captain Peter Townsend … mindful of the Church's teaching that Christian marriage is indissoluble and conscious of my duty to the Commonwealth, I resolved to put these considerations before others.'[18] Her personal sacrifice on behalf of the Church, the Commonwealth and, in part, her sister was now public. Churchill had previously arranged for Townsend to be posted to the British Embassy in Brussels in 1953 and it was there, in 1959, that he married a young Belgian woman named Marie-Luce Jamagne. On 6 May 1960, Margaret married society photographer Anthony Armstrong-Jones (later created Earl of Snowden) at Westminster Abbey.

In 2011, British prime minister David Cameron wrote to the leaders of the other Commonwealth Realms proposing an amendment to the Royal Marriages Act. The change would require only the first six family members in line to the throne to seek the sovereign's consent before marrying. Later that year, at the Commonwealth Heads of Government Meeting held in Perth, Australia, the proposed amendment was unanimously approved.

As dawn broke on Coronation Day, so too did the news that a British team had conquered Mount Everest. Captain John Hunt, Edmund Hillary and their Sherpa, Tenzing Norgay, became the first men to set foot on the world's highest summit. Back in England, despite meteorologists' predictions for sunny weather, grey skies loomed and a steady drizzle fell. Thirty thousand spectators spent a damp night camped along the processional route, and a further 3 million swarmed into London in the early hours. Seats in the stands were filled to capacity, and across the country people gathered around newly bought television sets. Churchill was staunchly opposed to televising the ceremony but Elizabeth went against the advice of her ministers, believing the nation had a right to participate. Only the most 'sacred' parts of the service – the anointing and communion – were performed without cameras present.

Personnel from all three branches of the military selected from countries spanning the Commonwealth lined the route to Westminster Abbey, the site of almost every British coronation since 1066. At 6 a.m., the abbey opened its doors to some 8,000 invited guests. Two hours later the procession of foreign royalty, heads of state and dignitaries began. At 11 a.m. the queen and the Duke of Edinburgh arrived in the Gold State Coach – originally built in 1762 and used at the coronation of every British monarch since George IV. Carrying St Edward's crown (made for Charles II in 1661), the lord high steward of England preceded Elizabeth into the abbey before the Archbishop of Canterbury, Geoffrey Fisher, announced her. And so commenced the three-hour service, watched by a 4-year-old Prince Charles seated in the royal box between his grandmother and aunt.

Once the oath was administered and communion conducted, the maids of honour removed Elizabeth's scarlet robe, gloves and jewels, and helped her don a simple white linen dress over her satin gown for her consecration. As she took her seat in St Edward's Chair, the choir sang *Zadok the Priest*, composed by Handel for the coronation of King George III. Under a silk canopy held in place by four Knights of the Garter, Fisher anointed Elizabeth with oil made from the same base as that used for her father's coronation seventeen years earlier. The queen was then invested with the Armills, Stole Royal, Robe Royal and Sovereign's Orb, followed by the Queen's Ring, the Sceptre with the Cross and the Sceptre with the Dove. Duly regaled, Queen Elizabeth II was crowned by the Archbishop of Canterbury. As St Edward's Crown was placed upon her head, the crowd chanted, 'God Save the Queen' three times.

Wearing the Imperial State Crown remade for the coronation of King George VI in 1937, and carrying the Sceptre with the Cross and Orb, Elizabeth left Westminster Abbey through the Great West Door for her return journey in the Gold State Coach. Bells rang and guns fired in salute. Joined by 2-year-old Princess Anne, the royal family made its final appearance of the day on the balcony at Buckingham Palace.

It is estimated that 27 million Britons tuned in to watch the coronation. The young queen's decision to televise the event proved a wise one.

4

The Reigning Queen

It is a complete misconception to imagine that the monarchy exists in the interests of the monarch. It doesn't. It exists in the interests of the people. If at any time any nation decides that the system is unacceptable, then it is up to them to change it.

Prince Philip, during a visit to Canada in 1969[19]

In November 1953, five months after the coronation, the queen and the Duke of Edinburgh embarked on a six-month tour of the Commonwealth. The trip, encompassing twelve countries – many of which had never before been visited by a reigning British monarch – was the most ambitious royal tour ever undertaken. It presented an opportunity to capitalise on the queen's popularity and solidify support for the monarchy across the Commonwealth. The couple travelled to five continents, covering 43,618 miles by land, air and sea. Once again, Charles and his sister Anne were left at home in the care of their grandmother, aunt and a team of nannies.

In 1983, Charles and Diana were much lauded for setting a new precedent by taking their 9-month-old son Prince William on their six-week tour to Australia and New Zealand. Pundits took to their columns, comparing the cold unfeeling queen who left her children behind, to Diana, who defied convention and broke with tradition. In order to do a fair comparison, however, one must consider the generational divide. Thirty years had passed between the queen's tour and that of the Waleses', during which time advances in modern aviation made travel significantly speedier. People's attitudes towards royalty had shifted and, popular as she was, Diana was merely a princess, not the queen. Following a seventeen-hour flight, Elizabeth's arrival in Bermuda, her first stop on the tour, was met by an Honour Guard, jubilant crowd and an array of dignitaries. News reports declared that nearly every one of the island nation's 38,000 residents had turned out for a glimpse of their new sovereign. In contrast, when Charles and Diana landed in Alice Springs, the first stop on their tour to Australia, there was not an Honour Guard or marching band to be seen, rather a handful of local officials waiting to greet them. After a brief photocall, William and his nanny departed for Woomargama, a working sheep and cattle ranch in South West Australia. William remained there for the duration of the tour, and his parents visited him nine times. In 2014, during their own three-week tour to Australia and New Zealand, William and Catherine spent only two nights away from their baby son, Prince George.

From Bermuda, Elizabeth and Philip moved on to Jamaica where they joined the royal yacht SS *Gothic*, which would be used for much of the tour. They sailed through the Panama Canal and on to Fiji and Tonga. By Christmas the couple had arrived in New Zealand, and it was from Government House in Auckland that the queen made the first Christmas address ever to have been broadcast from outside the United Kingdom. In February 1954, wearing her coronation gown, she opened the Australian parliament as queen of Australia, after which she spent two months travelling the length and breadth of the country. On 1 April, *Gothic* set sail for Ceylon (now Sri Lanka), making a one-day stop in the Cocos Islands, an Australian territory located in the Indian Ocean. Two weeks later the royal party travelled to Yemen, Uganda and Libya. During the final days of the tour, Charles and Anne joined HMY *Britannia*'s maiden voyage to Grand Harbour, Malta and Tobruk, Libya, where they reunited with their parents on 1 May. The family then sailed under full naval escort back across the Mediterranean Sea, returning to Malta on 3 May.

After a final stop in Gibraltar, *Britannia* was bound for England. On 15 May 1954 she cruised up the River Thames into London and under Tower Bridge, which was adorned with a vast welcome home sign. Amidst the deafening roar of ship sirens, the queen, Philip, Charles and Anne waved from the Royal Deck to the crowds lining the banks of the river before being met by the Queen Mother and Princess Margaret and returning home to Buckingham Palace.

If incessant news reports of Princess Margaret's doomed romance with Townsend had sullied the early days of Elizabeth's reign, the political situation over the subsequent decade only furthered the sense of disillusionment. In April 1955, Winston Churchill resigned. At his directive, the queen appointed Anthony Eden as his successor. Owing to his long wartime service, the deputy prime minister was a popular choice, but his tenure proved brief. In July 1956, Egyptian President Colonel Nasser seized the Suez Canal in response to America's withdrawal of its pledge to finance the construction of the Aswan Dam. A large percentage of the United Kingdom's oil supply passed through the canal, and international reaction to Nasser's actions was loud and vociferous across the political spectrum. Retaliation was swift. Israel invaded Egypt on 29 October 1956. Seven days later, on 5 November, having ignored the allies' call for a ceasefire, Egyptian forces were defeated when British and French paratroopers landed along the canal. Despite protestations to the contrary, it was clear that the Israeli offensive and Anglo-French attack had been a joint operation. What was not clear was how much Eden had disclosed to the queen prior to the invasion. While attending the Glorious Goodwood race meeting of 1956, Elizabeth was presented with a proclamation requiring her signature. The document, calling up the Army Reserve, led to Britain's disastrous involvement in the Suez affair. Pressure from the US, USSR and United Nations forced the three powers to withdraw. By the end of the year Anglo-French forces had pulled-out, though the canal did not reopen until April 1957. Lord Mountbatten claimed the queen was opposed to the invasion. Eden denied Mountbatten's assertions, but the humiliating failure in Egypt led to a rapid decline in Eden's health. In late November he flew to Jamaica to recuperate. He returned to London in mid-December looking healthy and rested, but he was not a well man and it was agreed that short-term breaks were not the long-term answer. Upon doctor's orders, Eden formally declared his resignation to the queen on 9 January 1957.

Since the execution of Charles I in 1649, the sovereign has remained politically neutral and acts purely on the advice of his or her ministers. It was, therefore, Lord Salisbury and Lord Kilmuir, Lord President and Lord

Chancellor respectively, who were tasked with conducting a cabinet-wide survey in order to name Eden's successor. After seeking their counsel, and that of Winston Churchill, the queen – in her symbolic role as head of state – appointed Harold Macmillan prime minister. R.A. Butler had been expected to replace Eden and, as a result, press reaction to the surprise announcement was immediate. The queen was castigated for allegedly allowing herself to be influenced by Tory aristocrats and elderly friends of her father, leading to a charge of favouritism. What was not made public was that she had also consulted with other respected elder statesmen and, in doing so, had upheld her duty in appointing a choice acceptable to Parliament. She faced similar criticism over the issue of royal prerogative in 1963. Heeding Harold Macmillan's advice upon his retirement, she named Lord Home prime minister and leader of the Conservative Party. The resulting controversy led the Conservatives to introduce an electoral procedure in 1965 ensuring a fair selection of future party leaders.

During her reign the queen has conducted weekly private audiences with twelve British prime ministers. David Cameron, the most recent, said of her, 'She asks brilliant, well-informed questions. She likes to know what's going on. She makes you think about what you are doing.'[20] It will be generations from now – when historians are granted access to Elizabeth's private diaries – that the public will learn of its sovereign's personal thoughts on her ministers, but there can be no doubt of her affection for Winston Churchill. In 1965, at the age of 90, the wartime leader died after suffering a stroke. An invaluable counsellor, he was Elizabeth's first prime minister and the first to be afforded a state funeral during her reign. The queen does not generally attend funerals of non-family members, preferring instead to send a representative in her place, but she has made exceptions. She was present for Churchill's service at St Paul's Cathedral where, upon her command, precedent was set aside in order to allow for his family members to arrive after and leave before her. In April 2013 she also attended the ceremonial funeral held for Margaret Thatcher, the country's first and only female prime minister to date.

In the autumn of 1956, Prince Philip set sail in the royal yacht for a solo four-month tour of the Commonwealth. The trip, viewed negatively by the general populace, was labelled 'Philip's Folly', and adverse reaction escalated due to his absence during the Suez Crisis and the resulting change in ministry. Rumours of a rift between Elizabeth and Philip increasingly made headlines – ever more so when the wife of Philip's equerry, Mike Parker, requested a divorce. Her decision prompted the palace to release a statement denying media speculation that Philip was the cause of the couple's separation. It was the beginning of the end of deference, and the media deemed the royal family fair game. The post-coronation honeymoon period was over.

In August 1957 the *National and English Review*, owned and edited by a young peer named Lord Altrincham, devoted an entire issue to the future of the monarchy. Altrincham declared the queen's court to be, 'A tight little enclave of English ladies and gentlemen.'[21] Her entourage out' of eligible young ladies, the queen was able to add an extra garden party to the royal calendar, allowing for 8,000 people from a broad spectrum of society to visit Buckingham Palace.

Though the latter part of the 1950s had been plagued by criticism, the '60s proved to be a personally happy time for the queen and Prince Philip. The couple's third child, Prince Andrew Albert Christian Edward, was born at Buckingham Palace on 19 February 1960. He was the first baby born to a reigning British monarch since the birth of Queen Victoria's youngest child, Princess Beatrice in 1857. Three months later Princess Margaret married Anthony Armstrong-Jones. The first major royal event since the coronation, it was declared 'the wedding of the decade' and an estimated 3 million people tuned in to watch the pageantry unfold on television. On 10 March 1964 the last of the queen's children, Prince Edward Antony Richard Louis, was also born at Buckingham Palace, a month shy of her 38th birthday. Throughout the remainder of the decade Elizabeth and Philip travelled extensively, the aim being to spread a positive royal ethos throughout the world. Their tour to Germany in 1965 was the first visit by a British monarch since May 1913, when King George V and Queen Mary had travelled to Berlin for the wedding of Kaiser Wilhelm II's daughter, Victoria Luise. With the outbreak of the First World War just over a year later, the occasion marked the last time George and his cousins, Wilhelm II and Tsar Nicholas II, would all be together.

On the political front, the 1960s and '70s bore witness to the accelerated decolonisation of Africa and the Caribbean. As more than twenty countries gained independence from Britain, members of the royal family fanned out across the globe to attend independence ceremonies, further boosting the profile of the Commonwealth. In contrast to the respect held for the queen by Commonwealth citizens, a majority of those across the United Kingdom remained indifferent. The queen's first Labour prime minister, Harold Wilson, came to power following the general election of 1964. He was a loyal supporter of the monarchy, but amidst the backdrop of the swinging '60s the institution was deemed dull and out of touch. To counter public apathy, the queen invited television cameras behind the palace walls for the first time. Months of filming resulted in *The Royal Family*, a fifty-minute documentary which revealed the off-duty queen as she had never been seen before: enjoying family breakfast, flipping through photograph albums with her children and buying ice-cream in the local village shop. Today, images of Prince Philip flipping sausages on the barbeque at Balmoral look rather stilted, but at the time the film revolutionised public opinion. The Windsors were no longer considered aloof and untouchable, but rather more ordinary and accessible. Watched by two-thirds of the population, the documentary aired a week before the 1969 televised investiture of Prince Charles as the Prince of Wales at Caernarfon in north-west Wales. It was shown several times, but at the end of the year Buckingham Palace withdrew it from public view, and the film in its entirety has remained off-limits ever since. Cameras were in place once again for the wedding of Princess Anne to Captain

Mark Phillips at Westminster Abbey in 1973. A precedent had been set; since the coronation, television cameras have captured virtually every major royal milestone.

The 1970s marked a decade of firsts for the royal family. In 1970, the queen attended her first Commonwealth Games in Edinburgh, Scotland. On the international stage she made an historic visit to communist Yugoslavia in 1972, the following year saw her travel to Ottawa for her first Commonwealth Heads of Government Meeting held outside Britain, and in 1979 she became the first British sovereign to travel to the Middle East. In 1977 she welcomed her first grandson, Peter Phillips, born to Princess Anne at St Mary's Hospital, Paddington. Upon her marriage, Anne had declined the queen's offer of a royal title for her husband, Mark Phillips. As a result their son Peter was the first legitimate grandchild of a monarch to be born without a style or courtesy title in over 500 years. In 1978, despite having two children, Princess Margaret became the first senior royal to divorce since Henry VIII. In 1979 Lord Louis Mountbatten, uncle to Prince Philip and mentor to Prince Charles, became the first member of the modern royal family to be assassinated. He died instantly when a bomb planted by the IRA exploded in his boat, *Shadow V*, in County Sligo, Ireland, also killing his 14-year-old grandson and a local boy. By the end of the decade the British public had elected Margaret Thatcher to succeed James Callaghan as the country's prime minister; for the first time in history Britain had a female head of state as well as a female head of government.

In 1977 the queen celebrated her Silver Jubilee, marking the 25th anniversary of her reign. Accompanied by Prince Philip, she embarked on tours to Western Samoa, Tonga, Fiji, New Zealand, Australia, Papua New Guinea, Canada and the West Indies. On the 17 May the couple set off from Glasgow, beginning a three-month tour of the United Kingdom and Northern Ireland. Visiting thirty-six counties in all, Elizabeth became the first monarch to have traversed so much of the country in such a short span of time. Central celebrations began on the 6 June when she lit a bonfire beacon in Windsor, beginning a chain of beacons across the country. The next day she rode in the Gold State Coach to St Paul's Cathedral for a service of Thanksgiving attended by heads of state from around the world. After the service, members of the royal family attended a lunch at the Guildhall, during which the queen made a speech declaring, 'When I was twenty-one I pledged my life to the service of our people and I asked for God's help to make good that vow. Although that vow was made during my salad days, when I was green in judgement, I do not regret or retract a word of it.' Street parties and parades were held across the Commonwealth and it is estimated that 500 million people worldwide watched the events unfold live on television. On 9 June a river progress emulating the ceremonial barge trips of Elizabeth I sailed up the Thames from Greenwich to Lambeth. The night culminated with a firework display, lighted carriage procession and a final balcony appearance at Buckingham Palace.

The Jubilee celebrations proved that the public's zest for the monarchy had been reignited ... but not across all echelons of society. A small anti-monarchist movement planned a 'Stuff-the-Jubilee' march to Buckingham Palace to proclaim the republic, but according to rally organiser Terry Liddle, only five people turned up. Punk band The Sex Pistols made more of a splash, releasing its single *God Save the Queen* to coincide with the festivities. The highly controversial song, which made it to number two in the charts, accused the monarchy of being a 'fascist regime'. For better or for worse, the monarchy continued to rock the zeitgeist.

5

The Tabloid Generation

When life seems hard, the courageous do not lie down and accept defeat; instead, they are all the more determined to struggle for a better future.

Elizabeth II, Christmas address to the Commonwealth, 2008[23]

In the wake of the tempestuous 1970s, a decade rife with nationwide strikes, protests and mounting threats from the IRA, the '80s marked a new dawn for the House of Windsor. Throughout the political unrest of the previous years the queen had largely maintained her public standing, but it was clear the institution as a whole was in need of a shake up. Now in his 30s, Prince Charles' romantic interests were increasingly making headlines. The world's most eligible bachelor was developing a reputation as a playboy, and behind palace walls talk turned to the need for Charles to settle down. Enter Lady Diana Spencer, the youngest daughter of the 8th Earl Spencer. Diana's elder sister Sarah first introduced the couple in 1977 and by 1980 their friendship had blossomed into romance. Diana was very comfortable within royal circles and knew the royal form. Her family home, Park House, was located within the grounds of the queen's Sandringham Estate in Norfolk, where she spent much of her childhood playing with princes Andrew and Edward but, as her relationship with Charles developed, the sudden press intrusion proved to be utterly overwhelming. The media were captivated by the demure, pretty, 19-year-old nursery school teacher. Photographers camped outside her London flat; binoculars and long lenses were trained on her every move and speculation over the couple's relationship regularly resulted in front page tabloid headlines.

The royal family believed Charles had picked a winner, but the queen was well aware that the media was creating an intolerable situation for Diana. In early 1981, at the behest of his wife, Prince Philip wrote to Charles urging his eldest son to make a decision: either marry Diana or break off the relationship in order to preserve her reputation. On the 24 February 1981 Charles and Diana formally announced their betrothal. When asked during their engagement interview if he was in love, Charles' response of 'whatever in love means'[24] was, perhaps, an early indication that he felt pressured into the marriage but, as far as the world was concerned, the fairy tale was just beginning.

Five months later, on 29 July, Charles and Diana were married at St Paul's Cathedral. Wearing an ivory silk taffeta gown with 25ft train designed by David and Elizabeth Emanuel, Diana was escorted down the aisle by her father. Following the service, officiated by the Archbishop of Canterbury, Robert Runcie, the couple returned to Buckingham Palace in an open-topped landau. Once there, they stepped onto the balcony to greet the assembled masses eagerly chanting 'kiss her'. The newlyweds obliged, granting the day's defining moment. Billed as the 'wedding of the century' it was, for the royals at least, a family occasion, albeit one watched by an estimated global television audience of 750 million.

With 2 million spectators expected to line the processional route from Buckingham Palace to St Paul's

Cathedral, security had posed a tremendous cause for concern. A few weeks prior to the wedding, during the annual Trooping the Colour ceremony on the 13 June, 17-year-old Marcus Serjeant aimed a starting pistol directly at the queen and fired six blanks before being restrained by police. The queen, a consummate equestrian, regained control of her startled horse and continued on to Horse Guards Parade. It was not the first time modern royal security had been called into question. In 1974, Princess Anne had survived a kidnap attempt as she and her husband returned to Buckingham Palace from a charity film screening. Though the attack on Anne led to an overhaul in the handling of royal protection, serious infractions continued to occur.

In the early hours of 9 July 1982, Michael Fagan, a 33-year-old unemployed labourer, prompted the greatest royal security breach of the twentieth century when he broke into the queen's bedroom at Buckingham Palace. Before reaching her bedside, Fagan triggered the alarm twice as he helped himself to a bottle of wine and wandered undisturbed around the palace. Police silenced both warnings, believing them to have sounded in error. The queen was reported to have calmly chatted to Fagan as she waited a full 8 minutes for help to arrive, but in an interview in 2012, Fagan claimed that she had left the room almost immediately, leaving him under the watch of an unarmed footman before being arrested. Fagan's break-in was considered a civil wrong as opposed to a criminal offence, and the only charges filed against him were for the theft of the wine. Those charges were later dropped when he agreed to a psychiatric evaluation and he spent the next six months in a secure hospital. Today, Scotland Yard keeps a 'Fixated Persons Index' and a list of credible known threats, but the royal family remains stoic when it comes to the subject of security, preferring it to be as invisible as possible, thereby allowing themselves to be more accessible to the people.

Since the coronation, the queen had been the royal family's star attraction, but lingering enthusiasm for the recent royal wedding and public fascination with Diana in particular led to an insatiable appetite for news of the younger generation. To satisfy the growing demand for royal stories, media organisations appointed designated court reporters, but it wasn't long before newspaper headlines turned from the romance of the wedding to the reality of war.

In response to Argentina's invasion and subsequent occupation of the Falkland Islands in the South Atlantic in April 1982, Prime Minister Margaret Thatcher ordered the assembly of a Royal Naval task force – led by HMS *Invincible* and HMS *Hermes* – in a bid to reclaim the island territory. As sovereign and head of the Commonwealth, the queen was inevitably involved, but she had another more personal interest in the conflict. Her second-born son, Prince Andrew, was a serving officer on board *Invincible*. Government ministers, anxious that the second-in-line to the throne would pose a prime enemy target, hoped to reassign him to a desk job for the duration of the war. Andrew was determined to go. With his mother's support, the prince remained with his ship, serving as a Sea King helicopter pilot. He took part in a number of flying missions including anti-submarine and anti-surface warfare, casualty evacuations, transport, and search and rescue missions. More notably he piloted the helicopter used as a decoy for an Exocet missile. On 14 June 1982, Argentina surrendered. The conflict had lasted seventy-four days, during which time 255 Britons and 649 Argentinians and 3 civilians lost their lives. Upon *Invincible*'s return to Portsmouth Harbour on 17 September, the queen, Prince Philip and Princess Anne waited alongside the families of other crew members to welcome the ship home.

The Falklands War was as divisive as any other. Argentina was chiefly supported by fellow Latin American countries and received arms from Libya, whereas the UK had the backing of the Commonwealth, European Economic Community and the United States. America's support proved that the 'special relationship' between the two countries (a phrase first coined by Churchill in a speech in 1944) remained strong. In early June 1982, President Ronald Reagan and his wife Nancy embarked on a state visit to the UK. They were invited to stay with the queen at Windsor Castle, becoming the first presidential couple to be granted such an opportunity. The following year Elizabeth and Philip paid a ten-day visit to the US, during which time the Reagans hosted them at their ranch in Santa Barbara, California. In 1989 the queen conferred an honorary knighthood on the former president, making him an Honorary Knight Grand Cross of the Most Honourable Order of the Bath – the highest honour afforded to foreigners. Reagan was one of only three presidents to be awarded the knighthood, the other two being Eisenhower and George H.W. Bush.

In keeping with a long line of royal women before her, Diana, Princess of Wales gave birth to her first child within a year of her marriage to Charles. With his father present, Prince William Arthur Philip Louis was born at St Mary's Hospital, Paddington, on 21 June 1982. Though not the first royal to be born in a hospital, he was the first direct heir born outside the family home. Two years later, on 15 September 1984, the Waleses welcomed their second son, Prince Henry Charles Albert David, popularly known as Prince Harry. Archaic as it seems, by providing 'an heir and a spare', Diana had fulfilled her most important royal duty.

On 13 March 1986 the palace formally announced the engagement of Prince Andrew to Sarah Ferguson, the daughter of Prince Charles' polo manager, Major Ronald Ferguson. Dubbed 'Fergie' by the press, she was the complete antithesis of the shy and refined Diana. A career girl with long ties to the royal family, her boisterous energy and mischievous demeanour were deemed a breath of fresh air. The marriage took place four months later at Westminster Abbey on 23 July. On the morning of the wedding, the queen made Andrew Duke of York, a title previously held by his maternal grandfather and great-grandfather. The couple's daughters, princesses Beatrice and Eugenie, were born in 1988 and 1990 respectively.

For Fleet Street's newspaper editors the new generation of royals were veritable catnip. The *Sun* labelled Diana the 'Queen of Hearts' and her every outfit, hairstyle and gesture dominated headlines. No celebrity or political figure before her had been covered so voraciously. During a special briefing at Buckingham Palace in 1981 Michael

Shea, the queen's press secretary, appealed to journalists to 'ease off'; following the meeting the assembled media were invited to join the queen and Prince Philip for a reception. The late William Deedes, former editor of the *Daily Telegraph*, later recounted:

> I was in a small group with the Queen when she observed, 'It's hard on a girl if she can't go to the local sweet shop without being cornered by photographers.' The then editor of the *News of the World*, Barry Askew, said rather plaintively: 'Why couldn't she send a footman for the sweets?' The Queen replied, 'I think that is the most pompous remark I have ever heard in my life'.[25]

Just two months later, in spite of the palace's plea, both the *Sun* and the *Daily Star* printed paparazzi photographs revealing a visibly pregnant Diana in a bikini while on holiday with Charles in the Bahamas. Press coverage reached unprecedented levels in 1983 when Charles and Diana, accompanied by baby William, embarked on their first official overseas tour to Australia and New Zealand. Where previously only a handful of photographers had accompanied royal parties on international trips, suddenly snappers from all over the world were vying for a place.

Though media focus generally remained on the younger set, the queen did not escape entirely unscathed. In July 1986, under the headline, 'Queen Dismayed by Uncaring Thatcher',[26] *The Sunday Times* published an article suggesting a royal rift with Downing Street.

The piece reported that Elizabeth was unhappy with a number of Margaret Thatcher's policies, finding her approach to be 'confrontational and socially divisive'. It went on to express the queen's alarm over high unemployment, riots and strikes, as well as her unease over the prime minister's cavalier attitude towards the Commonwealth and her refusal to impose sanctions against the apartheid regime in South Africa. Given the monarchy's need for political neutrality, the story was tremendously embarrassing. *The Sunday Times* refused to reveal its sources, but it later transpired that Michael Shea had been duped into speaking a little too freely to a reporter at the paper. Shea remained adamant that his remarks had been wildly misinterpreted, but a few months later he left the palace after accepting a position at Hanson PLC. To this day members of the royal household remain resolute in their belief that the queen would never say anything indiscreet to a member of staff, but it can also be said that no one behind palace walls has the authority to reveal the queen's personal opinions. Throughout her tenure Margaret Thatcher remained a steadfast monarchist. Upon her resignation in 1990, the queen bestowed a personal gift on her former prime minster, appointing Thatcher to the Order of Merit and later to the Order of the Garter.

As embarrassing as *The Sunday Times* debacle had been, the self-inflicted misery of *It's a Royal Knockout* was infinitely worse. Following his graduation from Cambridge, Prince Edward enlisted with the Royal Marines, but after only four months of basic training

Buckingham Palace issued a brief statement declaring the prince's decision to resign. Edward, the first member of the modern royal family to quit military training, had concluded that he didn't wish to make the service his long-term career. His father, Prince Philip, Captain General of the Marines, was said to be furious, but Edward remained undeterred, eager to make his mark in a different arena. His opportunity came in the summer of 1987 when he convinced his siblings to serve as team leaders for a charity edition of *It's a Knockout*, a televised game show in which rival teams donned fancy dress and competed in an array of slapstick-style challenges. The Waleses declined to take part, but backed by a host of big-name celebrities, the Princess Royal and the Duke and Duchess of York agreed to participate.

The programme raised over 1 million pounds for charity, but undignified images of the young royals clad in brightly coloured mock-Tudor costumes, cheering on fellow teammates dressed as giant leeks and potatoes proved to be too much for the British public. The whole endeavour backfired spectacularly and criticism was harsh. It's often been asked why the queen did not intervene and put a stop to the idea, but she is not in the business of running a dictatorship and often finds it difficult to say no to her children. The royals' popularity had been on a steady upward trajectory since the marriage of Charles and Diana, but the fallout caused by *It's a Knockout* became a tipping point. The downward spiral had begun.

The 1980s had been halcyon years for the monarchy. The decade saw two large-scale royal weddings and the birth of five more grandchildren. In 1982, in her capacity as the head of the Church of England, the queen received Pope John Paul II – the first reigning pope to visit Britain in 450 years – at Buckingham Palace. Elizabeth and Philip undertook twenty-three state visits and embarked on forty-one trips to Commonwealth nations, including a 1988 tour to Australia in celebration of the country's bicentennial. Though Jamaica had chosen to remain a Commonwealth Realm – thereby retaining the queen as head of state – the country marked the 21st anniversary of its independence in 1983. The same year, Elizabeth travelled to the Caribbean nation to open the Jamaican parliament. Having turned sixty in 1986, the age of retirement for many, it was business as usual for Her Majesty. In 1990 she attended commemorations honouring the 50th anniversary of the Battle of Britain. No sooner had she observed the memory of one war, so her government primed the country for another. In February 1991, following the Iraqi invasion of Kuwait, British forces deployed to the Middle East to assist in the Allied action. The Gulf War, in which 569 coalition lives were lost, served as a pre-cursor to what would prove to be the most damaging and tumultuous decade of the queen's reign … the 1990s.

6

Annus Horribilis

It has always been easy to hate and destroy. To build and to cherish is much more difficult.

Elizabeth II, first televised Christmas address to the Commonwealth, 1957[27]

Following the Allied victory in the Gulf, the international community developed a renewed sense of interest in the British monarchy. In May 1991 the queen became the first British head of state to address a joint meeting of the US Congress in Washington. Her speech, frequently interrupted by enthusiastic applause, thanked Americans for ' their steadfast loyalty to our common enterprise throughout this turbulent century'.[28] With a non-partisan approach, the queen was able to emphasise the importance of the Allied peacekeeping force. The value of her role as a ceremonial ambassador had been reinforced.

Back at home, stories on the high-profile lives of the Waleses and Yorks were splashed across the front pages of Britain's daily newspapers with startling regularity. As a result, the queen and Prince Philip had all but faded into obscurity. With another landmark anniversary approaching, it was decided that the time was right for a new behind-the-scenes style documentary in the vein of the 1969 film *The Royal Family*. Aides believed the public should be reminded of the true purpose of the monarchy, in contrast to the royal soap opera being played out in the media. From mid-1990 to late 1991 the BBC was granted remarkable access to the family during a period that included the queen's first meeting with Nelson Mandela at a Commonwealth summit in Zimbabwe, a state visit to the US, an unannounced official visit to Northern Ireland, a G7 summit and preparations at Windsor Castle for a three-day state visit by Polish president Lech Walesa. The documentary also revealed intimate footage of private family gatherings at Balmoral, and Elizabeth and her mother attending Derby Day at Epsom Downs Racecourse. The queen has never granted a formal interview; her likes, dislikes, opinions and political leanings can only be speculated upon so the film's real coup was Elizabeth's vocal commentary in which she offered relaxed, personal insights into her role. She spoke of receiving letters, giving honours and providing the entertainment for foreign guests. Referring to the infamous 'red boxes' filled with matters of state she said, 'Most people have a job and then they go home. In this existence the job and the life go on together. The boxes and the communications just keep on coming.'[29] Of Balmoral, the family's oft-professed sanctuary, she observed, 'It's rather nice to hibernate.' An estimated 30 million people tuned in to watch the award-winning *Elizabeth R*, which aired on 6 February 1992, the 40th anniversary of the queen's accession.

In February 1992, Charles and Diana embarked on a joint tour to India. Speculation over the state of their marriage was in overdrive and further fuelled when Diana was photographed alone in front of the Taj Mahal, the world's most iconic symbol of love. On an earlier visit to the ancient monument in 1980, Prince Charles had vowed to one day return with the woman he loved. The fact that he did not return with Diana was not lost on the accompanying press pack. Instead, he had chosen to attend an international business leaders forum 1,200 miles away in Bangalore.

With Andrew away at sea, the Duchess of York had fallen in with a raucous crowd, and was frequently spotted on the arm of Texan oil tycoon, Steve Wyatt. Following publication of photographs of the two on holiday in the Mediterranean, rumours of a romance began to surface. Though hotly denied by Andrew and Sarah, the couple announced their separation on 19 March 1992. In April, the already separated Princess Anne and Captain Mark Phillips finalised their divorce. In May, Fergie moved out of Sunninghill Park, the marital home she shared with Prince Andrew, taking their daughters with her. By August she was back on the front pages with the release of topless photographs of her lying poolside in the South of France with John Bryan, her 'financial advisor', further alienating her from the royal family. But it was *The Sunday Times* serialisation of *Diana: Her true Story*, by former tabloid journalist Andrew Morton on the 7 June, that instantly ignited a royal firestorm.

The publication of Morton's book single-handedly changed the face of royal journalism. The queen was not directly criticised, but the Windsor family did not fare well. The book provided lurid accounts of Diana's alleged eating disorders, suicide attempts and private misery. Most damning of all were the revelations of Charles' 'secret friendship' with Camilla Parker Bowles. The Chairman of the Press Complaints Committee, Archbishop of Canterbury, MPs and fellow members of the press all denounced the book based on their belief that Diana would never speak to an ex-tabloid reporter. Regardless, the book sold 2 million copies within the first two months of its publication. Diana denied any involvement, but she had secretly cooperated with Morton by providing tape-recorded answers to his questions. Though she deeply regretted her actions, Diana had intentionally betrayed the royal family's trust.

The press, believing it had been conned for the better part of ten years, no longer took Buckingham Palace at its word. The royals were considered fair game and tapes of private conversations, which had been around for years, resurfaced. In August the *Sun* published transcripts of a telephone exchange between Diana and her long-time friend James Gilbey, reportedly recorded on New Year's Eve 1989, in which he affectionately referred to her as 'Squidgy'. Not to be outdone, the *Daily Mirror* retaliated three months later, printing a humiliating and explicit conversation between Charles and his mistress, Camilla Parker Bowles. The queen was not responsible for her children's mounting woes, but as head of both the family and the institution, the mantle of blame lay heavily on her shoulders.

Amidst the relentless tabloid scourge, Charles and Diana's unified pretence continued. In November they embarked on a diplomatically successful tour to South Korea, but it would prove to be their last official overseas visit together. Under the glare of the international spotlight the public veneer finally cracked, and it was obvious that marital relations had irrevocably broken down. On 9 December, less than a month after their return, Prime Minister John

Major announced to the House of Commons that the couple had agreed to separate. Unlike the breakdown of the two royal marriages earlier in the year, the Waleses' separation immediately raised constitutional concerns. In his statement Major insisted that 'Their Royal Highnesses have no plans to divorce and their constitutional positions are unaffected. This decision has been reached amicably and they will both continue to participate fully in the upbringing of their children.'[30] An agreement had been reached, but Diana's absence from the royal family Christmas two weeks later, the first away from her boys, was indicative of how delicate the balance really was.

The year had been an unmitigated disaster for the monarchy, and the fire at Windsor Castle presented one more paralysing setback. It started on the morning of 20 November when a halogen lamp ignited a curtain in the queen's private chapel. Due to on-going construction, most of the furniture and artwork housed in the castle had been placed in storage, but the fire caused extensive damage to more than 100 rooms. Prince Andrew, who was on hand to help in the rescue effort, gave an impromptu news conference in which he described his mother as 'shocked and devastated'. Images of the forlorn monarch clad in a raincoat and headscarf as she watched the blaze unfold led to a wave of public sympathy, but it was short-lived. As the last of the embers were extinguished, talk turned to who would pay for the restoration. Given that the castle was uninsured, Heritage Secretary Peter Brooke stated that the Government would foot the bill, estimated to be £40 million. The outcry was immediate. After years of reports citing marital strife, the queen's tax immunity and the excesses of the 'free-loading' hangers-on, Brooke had misjudged the mood of the nation, and the press eagerly fanned the flames of disgust.

The queen's tax exemption was not a result of ancient privilege, but rather due to a policy set in place only half a century earlier. In the wake of Edward VIII's abdication, George VI incurred enormous expense compensating his brother, who had no personal wealth of his own. In order to meet those costs Prime Minister Neville Chamberlain agreed to a tax deal, believing its push through Parliament would invite less attention than a new arrangement for the Civil List. Upon her accession, the queen simply inherited the system.

In April 1989 the *Sunday Times* published its first 'Rich List'. In the absence of any official figures accounting for the queen's private wealth, Elizabeth – regularly portrayed as the multi-billionaire owner of the royal yacht, queen's flight, royal train, Crown Jewels and priceless Royal Collection – predictably came in at number one. In point of fact the queen does not own any of them, nor does she own the many royal castles and palaces scattered throughout the UK. The Sandringham Estate in Norfolk and Balmoral Castle in Scotland are her private residences, but everything else is held in trust for the nation. Two years after the list was published the queen tumbled to a more realistic number fifty-nine; by 2014 she had fallen to 285, and in 2015 she dropped out of the top 300.

Nevertheless, in 1992 demands made by a recession-weary public had reached fever pitch. What it didn't know was that extensive household reforms instigated by Lord Airlie, the Lord Chamberlain, upon his appointment to the palace in 1984, had led to a significant overhaul in the royal finances. Airlie spearheaded a number of radical changes resulting in the implementation of a more efficient, cost-effective system. By February 1992 aides felt confident that the queen could afford to pay taxes, and the palace entered into discussions with the Inland Revenue Service. In a statement to the House of Commons on 26 November, the prime minister announced that the queen and Prince Charles would voluntarily begin to pay tax on their private incomes the following April. He also declared that the queen had further agreed to cut Civil List payments to five other members of the royal family. The overwhelming impression was that the queen had bowed to tabloid pressure but, as the prime minister went on to say, the decision had been made directly by Her Majesty almost a year earlier.

Elizabeth remained resolutely silent throughout what had been a trying year. Her only reference was made during a speech at a Guildhall luncheon on 24 November, celebrating the anniversary of her sovereignty. Nursing laryngitis and a heavy cold, she stated, '1992 is not a year on which I shall look back with undiluted pleasure. In the words of one of my more sympathetic correspondents, it has turned out to be an *Annus Horribilis*.'[31] Perhaps as a rebuke to some of the more unscrupulous reporters, she added:

There can be no doubt, of course, that criticism is good for people and institutions that are part of public life. No institution – City, Monarchy, whatever – should expect to be free from the scrutiny of those who give it their loyalty and support, not to mention those who don't. But we are all part of the same fabric of our national society and that scrutiny, by one part of another, can be just as effective if it is made with a touch of gentleness, good humour and understanding.

Some believed the speech to be a cry for help, others thought it an act of penance, but at the very least it could be seen as a call for common sense and reason to be restored.

December offered a brief respite from the doom and gloom when, upon her marriage to Timothy Laurence, a commander in the Royal Navy, Princess Anne became the first royal divorcée to marry since Queen Victoria's granddaughter, Victoria, Grand Duchess of Hesse and by Rhine. Prince Philip escorted his daughter down the aisle of Crathie Kirk, a small church near Balmoral in Scotland, and the wedding was attended by Anne's children, Peter and Zara, as well as other members of the royal family. Like Phillips before him, Laurence received no royal title, but in 2007 he was made a Companion of the Order of Bath and, in 2011, the queen awarded him a KCVO, which he had earned in his own right as vice admiral in the Royal Navy.

After the divorce of one child and the separation of two others, a devastating fire at her favourite official residence, an explosive tell-all book and an unprecedented level of public scrutiny, the queen was to be dealt a final blow before year's end. Two days prior to its airing, the *Sun*, choosing to disregard embargo rules, printed the full text of the queen's Christmas Day message. In doing so, the impact of the speech in which the queen spoke of putting her worries into perspective and underlined her family's commitment to service, was greatly reduced. The queen was described officially as 'very, very distressed' by the *Sun*'s actions and, in an unusual move, the palace sued for breach of copyright. Initially it looked as though the paper was set to fight the charge, but in a rare royal victory, the *Sun* agreed to pay legal costs as well as £200,000 to charity.

As her Christmas Day message drew to a close the queen said, '1993 will certainly bring new challenges, but let us resolve to meet it with fresh hope in our hearts. There is no magic formula that will transform sorrow into happiness, intolerance into compassion or war into peace, but inspiration can change human behaviour.'[32] Her words served as a call for the troubles of 1992 to finally be laid to rest.

7

Death of Diana

She loves her duty and means to be a Queen and not a puppet.

Prime Minister Harold Macmillan, November 1961[33]

The period following the fire at Windsor Castle had been a bruising one for the monarchy and the question of who would pay for the restoration continued to loom large. In April 1993, Lord Airlie announced that the State Rooms at Buckingham Palace would be opened to the paying public during the summer months as part of a five-year experimental plan designed to raise the necessary funds. Furthermore, Windsor Castle was to begin charging a fee for admission to the grounds. The venture proved a success. During the allotted time period seventy per cent of the estimated £40 million restoration budget was secured. Once repairs were completed in 1997, costs totalled £37 million – 3 million under budget.

Annually, more than 50,000 people are invited to attend events at Buckingham Palace, from state banquets and garden parties to investitures and receptions, but the idea of opening the palace – inspired by the queen and endorsed by Prince Philip – was a royal first. Billed by the media as a revolutionary step, the palace opened its doors to the public on 3 August 1993. The inaugural season was a tremendous success, and the annual summer exhibition remains a popular attraction to this day. Between them, Buckingham Palace and Windsor Castle welcome 1.4 million visitors per annum, and in turn generate £22 million in admission fees and retail sales combined. Once costs have been met, the remainder of the money raised supports the work of the Royal Collection. Estimated to contain over 1 million items, the Royal Collection is one of the largest private art collections in the world. Held in trust for the nation, it receives no government funding.

As the early 1990s continued to be dominated by headlines analysing every sorry detail of the 'War of the Waleses', the queen was busy building bridges and solidifying new relationships on the international stage. In October 1994, she and Prince Philip visited Russia following the election of Boris Yeltsin, the country's first democratic leader. Despite close family ties to former tsars, Elizabeth became the first British monarch to set foot in Moscow's Red Square. In March 1995 she returned to South Africa for her first visit to the country since the tour of 1947. On hand to welcome her was newly elected President Nelson Mandela, who had overseen his country's return to the Commonwealth after an absence of thirty-three years. In the wake of the fall of communism in Eastern Europe, the nineties also bore witness to the queen's historic visits to Hungary, Poland and the Czech Republic. Back at home, the summer of 1995 gave way to festivities marking the 50th anniversaries of VE and VJ Day. Joined by her 95-year-old mother and her sister Margaret, the queen waved to the crowds from the balcony of Buckingham Palace, where they had stood half a century earlier marking the end of the Second World War. For a brief moment the common bond of national pride restored a sense of unity between the monarchy and the people.

The opening of Buckingham Palace was a step in the right direction in terms of restoring goodwill, but the monarchy continued to suffer from the damaging effects of the previous year. In an effort to counter the negativity spawned by the Morton book, Prince Charles' office worked diligently towards rebranding its principal. In 1994 the prince granted a candid interview to journalist Jonathan Dimbleby. The resulting two-and-a-half-hour film, *Charles: The Private Man, The Public Role*, depicting Charles as an earnest, hardworking royal, was designed to focus on the achievements of the Prince's Trust. While it did present a compelling view into the prince's role as a public figure, the central theme was overshadowed by Charles's admission that he had been unfaithful to his wife after his marriage had 'irretrievably broken down'.[34] Was Charles the first royal to be unfaithful? No … but he was the first to admit it before a television audience of 14 million. His confession of adultery, delivered on camera while seated in the choir stalls of St George's Chapel, Windsor, begged the overriding question: was the prince fit to succeed? Further damning was the subsequent publication of *The Prince of Wales*, Dimbleby's accompanying book, authorised by Charles. Serialised in *The Sunday Times*, it alluded to the prince's unhappy childhood, gave voice to his version of events surrounding his turbulent marriage and delved further into his relationship with 'good friend' Camilla Parker Bowles. In an instant, Charles eradicated any remaining semblance of public sympathy.

On the 20 November 1995, 23 million Britons tuned in to see Diana deliver her final retaliatory shot. 'There were three of us in this marriage so it was a bit crowded,'[35] she professed to reporter Martin Bashir in an interview for the BBC's current affairs programme, *Panorama*. She questioned Charles' suitability for the throne and, perhaps as a final challenge to the House of Windsor, she stated that she would like to be known as 'Queen of People's Hearts'. The interview had been so covert that nobody within the royal household knew anything about it. Even Lord Hussey, chairman of the BBC governors, whose wife Lady Susan served as a lady-in-waiting to the queen, had been kept in the dark. The queen had strived to be supportive of Diana, but after such a scathing betrayal it was impossible to continue. In December she wrote to both Charles and Diana informing them that, after lengthy discussions with the Archbishop of Canterbury and the prime minister, it was her wish that the two finally divorce. Six months later, on 28 August 1996, upon a joint custody agreement, financial settlement and the removal of HRH from Diana's formal title, the divorce was finalised. Nobody could have predicted that a year and three days later Diana, Princess of Wales would be dead.

In the early hours of Sunday, 31 August 1997, 36-year-old Diana, her friend Dodi Fayed and their chauffeur Henri Paul were killed when their car crashed in the Pont d'Alma Tunnel in Paris while trying to elude the paparazzi. As Britons awoke to the news, the overriding sense was one of shock and disbelief. Lingering sympathy for the princess and her enduring popularity led to unprecedented levels of public mourning. Blame for her death was initially levelled against the press, and culpability was further cemented when Diana's brother, Earl Spencer, stated that every editor who had published intrusive pictures of Diana had blood on their hands. Emotions were running high, and the events of the ensuing week would prove the single greatest test of the queen's reign.

Before dawn, members of the public began their pilgrimages to Kensington and Buckingham palaces to lay flowers. In Scotland the royal family, accompanied by princes William and Harry, attended its regular Sunday morning worship service at Crathie Kirk but, in what was perceived as the first of many confounding blunders, there was no reference to Diana during the service. The chaplain, Reverend Robert Sloan, explained that he had not mentioned the princess out of concern for her sons, but his omission later fuelled the notion that the Windsors simply didn't care. The recently elected Labour prime minister Tony Blair who had come to power following a landslide victory the previous May, also attended church that morning. In an emotional speech beforehand he referred to Diana as the 'People's Princess'. As the week progressed, his sentimentality, set against the backdrop of the royal family's stoic silence, served only to seal the public's tabloid-driven rage aimed at its absentee monarch and the glaringly bare flagpole atop Buckingham Palace.

Of immediate concern to palace aides was the repatriation of Diana's body. Following the Sunday morning church service, Charles flew to Paris with Diana's two sisters, returning to RAF Northolt with the princess' casket just before 7 p.m. Diana's brother, Earl Spencer, expressed his wish for Buckingham Palace to organise a royal funeral. The palace has plans in place for every sort of royal funeral and internal rehearsals are regularly conducted, but with no blueprint for the funeral of a non-royal mother of the future king, the Lord Chamberlain's office was left with a blank slate. A funeral committee was established, chaired by Lord Airlie. Working closely with the clergy, commissioner of the Metropolitan Police and members of the royal household, it was decided that Diana's funeral would take place on Saturday, 6 September at Westminster Abbey. Her coffin was to be carried on a gun carriage drawn by the King's Troop Royal Horse Artillery, and 500 representatives of the princess' charities were to march behind the cortège. To aid crowd control the processional route was extended to begin at Kensington Palace as opposed to St James's Palace, and giant screens were erected in Hyde Park and Regent's Park to ease congestion. As plans were hastily set in motion, the queen's refusal to return to London, her failure to address the nation and the lack of flag flying at half-mast above Buckingham Palace became sources of increasing public disquiet.

The queen was in regular daily contact with Buckingham Palace but, firmly ensconced at Balmoral, it was impossible to grasp the true extent of the mounting hostility. Bound by tradition and caught between her desire to protect her grandsons and meet the demands of the public, her perceived lack of emotion led to accusatory headlines labelling her 'remote' and 'insensitive'. 'Speak to us Ma'am,' begged the *Mirror*. 'Show us you care,' challenged the *Sun*. Nevertheless, the flag was a point on which the queen refused to budge.

Since the reign of Queen Victoria, tradition has dictated that the Royal Standard, the flag that bears the sovereign's arms, fly at Buckingham Palace whenever the sovereign is in residence, and that in her absence no other flag should be flown. When the reigning monarch dies, the heir automatically accedes. On that basis the Royal Standard never flies at half-mast. Furthermore, the Union Flag never flies at the palace. Had it been Philip or Charles who had died the same rules would have applied, but the grieving public was not interested in the minutiae of tradition. For the thousands of people queuing to sign the books of condolence at St James's Palace, many of them for upwards of five hours, the vacant flagpole at Buckingham Palace represented a monarchy distinctly out of touch.

On the day of Diana's funeral the queen conceded and, at her directive, the Union Flag flew at half-mast. Since then it has regularly been flown in the queen's absence, just as it does at her other official residences. It was lowered to half-mast upon the death of Queen Elizabeth The Queen Mother, as a mark of respect following the 9/11 attacks in the US and once again in the wake of the 7/7 bombings in London. On the first anniversary of Diana's death, the flag was lowered in tribute to the princess.

On Thursday, 4 September Prince Charles returned to London with princes William and Harry. The trio paid a visit to Kensington Palace to view the ever-expanding carpet of flowers. Aged 15 and 12 respectively, the boys' composure before a sea of weeping onlookers was astonishing. The queen and Prince Philip made their own highly anticipated return to London the next day. After viewing the books of condolence and greeting well-wishers at the gates to Buckingham Palace, Elizabeth delivered a live address to the nation, broadcast at 6 p.m. from the Chinese Dining Room. Typically, the queen only addresses the nation during her annual Christmas Day message but, recognising the needs of the people, she set precedent aside and paid tribute to Diana. She described the princess as someone she admired and respected, and acknowledged that there were 'lessons to be drawn' from her life. 'What I say to you now, as your queen and as a grandmother, I say from my heart,'[36] she continued. 'This week at Balmoral, we have all been trying to help William and Harry come to terms with the devastating loss that they and the rest of us have suffered.' In an instant the illusion of an aloof and reclusive queen was dispelled. It had been a week in which Elizabeth was berated as never before, but perhaps historians will note it as the only week of her reign in which she chose family before duty.

The following morning, as the abbey's minute bell marked the progress of Diana's funeral procession, the queen led her family to the North Gate of Buckingham Palace. As the cortège drew level, the woman who bows before no one lowered her head in reverence to Diana. It was a symbolic gesture, but one that spoke of humility. It had been a trying week, but the people had spoken and the queen had listened.

In October 1997 Elizabeth embarked on a state visit to Pakistan and India. The tour, marking fifty years since independence from British rule, was designed to cement relations between the nations but instead became a trip marred by diplomatic failure. British Foreign Secretary Robin Cook remarked that he favoured an international mediation between India and Pakistan in their dispute over Kashmir, a matter which Indian officials had deemed an internal affair. On the eve of her arrival in New Delhi, Indian prime minister Inder Gujral, so enraged by Cook's comments, described the queen as the leader of a 'third-rate nation'. The British press laid blame for her disastrous reception entirely on Cook's shoulders, and it was left to the queen to diffuse further tensions. During her visit to Amritsar, Indian protesters called on the queen to formally apologise for the 1919 massacre of hundreds of unarmed Indians by British troops. Though she fell short of apologising for one of the worst atrocities committed by the British on Indian soil, she removed her shoes before laying a wreath and paying silent homage to the 379 people who lost their lives at the site of the tragedy. Although the queen was not held accountable for the tour's catalogue of diplomatic errors, it was an inauspicious start to her official return to duties following the death of Diana.

Elizabeth and Philip's Golden Wedding Anniversary on 20 November 1997 finally offered an opportunity for celebration. Though the mood of the nation was still somewhat sombre, it was decided that the occasion should be marked, given that Elizabeth was the first reigning sovereign to reach such a milestone since George III in 1811. The day prior to their anniversary, Prince Philip delivered a speech at a Guildhall luncheon in which he shared the secret to a happy marriage, 'You can take it from me that the queen has the quality of tolerance in abundance.'[37] The next day a service of Thanksgiving was held at Westminster Abbey, followed by lunch hosted by the prime minister. With invited guests drawn from all walks of life, the lunch was invariably labelled 'the people's lunch', alluding to Blair's reference to Diana as the 'People's Princess'. During her address the queen paid tribute to her husband, saying, 'He is someone who doesn't take easily to compliments but he has, quite simply, been my strength and stay all these years, and I, and his whole family, and this and many other countries, owe him a debt greater than he would ever claim, or we shall ever know.'[38] In his remarks, Blair spoke of the queen being unstuffy, unfussy and unfazed by anything. In conclusion he said, 'You are our Queen. We respect and cherish you. You are, simply, the Best of British.'[39] Though his words received a mixed response, the Golden Anniversary celebration helped restore the queen and Prince Philip's image as steadfast pillars of the monarchy. With 'lessons to be drawn' as the recurring theme, it was time for a new monarchy, under Labour's 'New Britain' and, with a new millennium on the horizon, a tentative recovery was finally underway.

8

History in the Making

In this special year, as I dedicate myself anew to your service, I hope that we will all be reminded of the power of togetherness and the convening strength of family friendship and good neighbourliness.

Elizabeth II, Accession Day Statement, February 2012[40]

In the months following Diana's death, Buckingham Palace hired a communications director to oversee the restoration of the royal image. The palace adopted a less formal approach to official engagements, while aides strived to think creatively in terms of their orchestration. Themed away-days were established, allowing for visits devoted to a particular industry or profession. One of the first revolved around London's theatre community. In the spring of 1999 the queen visited young performers at the National Theatre and Angel's Costumiers in the West End, before meeting students at the Royal Academy of Dramatic Art. In the evening she and Prince Philip attended a performance of *Oklahoma!* – a nostalgic choice given that it was the first musical she ever saw back in 1947. The audience, unaware that royalty would be present, erupted in spontaneous applause upon the couple's arrival. The day was a hit, and away-days of varying themes became a permanent fixture on the royal calendar.

Modernisation was not just occurring within the monarchy. After assuming power in May 1997, New Labour was awash with reformist ideas. One of the first entities to feel the pinch was HMY *Britannia*, considered by many a symbol of 'Old' Britain. Though originally commissioned by a Labour prime minister, Clement

Attlee, the evolution of royal air travel rendered *Britannia* semi-redundant, and the government concluded that it could no longer justify her expense. After forty-four years of service *Britannia* was decommissioned in December 1997. In a rare show of vulnerability, the queen was seen to shed a tear during the ship's decommissioning ceremony. For the royals, *Britannia* was more than a successful international trade platform; she was a family home filled with treasured memories and provided a personal sanctuary where Elizabeth was untouchable. Her retirement marked the end of a royal era, but today, docked in the Port of Leith in Scotland, *Britannia* remains a popular tourist attraction.

In September 1998 the queen and Prince Philip embarked on a state visit to Brunei, before travelling to Kuala Lumpur, where they were to open the Commonwealth Games. During the trip Elizabeth was photographed travelling in a commuter train. Her speeches were dotted with buzzwords such as 'modernisation' and 'change', and, while on a visit to a Kuala Lumpur shopping centre, she signed footballs for Malaysian Manchester United fans. The trip, designed to showcase the monarch's new hands-on approach, was heralded a success.

The queen's youngest son Edward married public relations executive Sophie Rhys-Jones at St George's Chapel, Windsor, in June 1999. Broadcast live around the world, the wedding was low-key in its approach and suited the nation's mood perfectly. Unlike the weddings of the 1980s, the country did not come to a standstill, and expectations of fairy-tale endings had been resigned to the previous decade. In a break with tradition Edward was created Earl of Wessex upon his marriage, as opposed to being granted a royal dukedom, but it is widely believed that upon Charles' accession, he will inherit his father's title, the Duke of Edinburgh.

Sorrow overshadowed the early months of the queen's Golden Jubilee year in 2002. After years of poor health and debilitating strokes, Princess Margaret died on 9 February, three days after Accession Day. Weeks later, on 30 March, with Elizabeth by her side, the Queen Mother passed away at Royal Lodge, her home in the grounds of Windsor Great Park, at the age of 101. An estimated 200,000 people queued, many of them for over twenty-four hours, for a chance to pay their respects as Queen Elizabeth The Queen Mother lay in state at Westminster Hall.

Despite the response to the deaths of Elizabeth's mother and sister, the press argued that the British public no longer cared about the monarchy, and as such the Jubilee celebrations would be a flop. During the course of the year the queen and Prince Philip travelled over 40,000 miles, visiting a broad section of the UK and embarking on tours to Commonwealth Realms. Central celebrations stretched over a four-day weekend in June and included a classical music concert, *Prom at the Palace* – the largest event ever held within the grounds of Buckingham Palace. A follow-up concert, *Party at the Palace*, showcased the achievements of fifty years of pop music. More than 1 million people watched on giant screens erected along the Mall as guitarist Brian May strummed God Save the Queen from the roof of the palace. On 4 June the entire royal family attended a National Service of Thanksgiving at St Paul's Cathedral to which the queen rode in the Gold State Coach. Following an afternoon procession of floats depicting fifty years of British life and a parade of representatives from the [then] fifty-four member states of the Commonwealth of Nations marching in national dress, the royal family assembled on the balcony of Buckingham Palace. Contrary to the media's gloomy predictions, the Jubilee had been a resounding hit.

Emulating the toned-down style of his younger brother's wedding, Prince Charles chose Windsor for his marriage to Camilla Parker Bowles in April 2005. Given the issue of divorce on both sides, the couple were married in a civil ceremony in Windsor Town Hall. In her capacity as supreme governor of the Church of England (which refused to marry couples for whom adultery was a factor in the breakdown of their original marriage), the queen did not attend the civil proceedings, but she was present for the couple's subsequent service at St George's Chapel during which Charles and Camilla recanted their sins before being blessed. Out of respect for Diana's memory, it was announced that Camilla would take her style from Charles' ducal titles and be known as HRH The Duchess of Cornwall. Married as she was to the Prince of Wales, she would never be known as the Princess of Wales. Nevertheless, Charles' happiness and William and Harry's apparent approval of their new step-mother thawed much of the public animosity towards Camilla.

In contrast, the wedding of Prince William to Catherine Middleton at Westminster Abbey on 29 April

2011 captivated both the nation and the world. Fourteen years on from Diana's death, less emphasis had been put on William's finding an appropriate virgin, and more on the necessity of his finding a spouse suited to the demands of royal life. The couple met while students at St Andrew's University. Due to a 1995 agreement between the palace and the media, which granted William his privacy for the duration of his education in exchange for regular updates, the couple were largely able to court free of press intrusion. Not the first commoner to marry a direct heir, Catherine was certainly the most middle class and, unlike Diana, she was the product of a secure and happy childhood. Having dated for over eight years, many of those spent co-habiting, Catherine had an acute understanding of the role she was to fulfil and, perhaps more importantly, she had an unyielding protector in William. On their wedding day the queen bestowed William a dukedom. The couple would be known as the Duke and Duchess of Cambridge.

The global hysteria surrounding William and Catherine's wedding, led to the couple being credited for the monarchy's resurgence in popularity, but it was the changes set in motion over a decade earlier that created an institution better able to adapt to the expectations of the nation. Financial reforms had resulted in the removal of minor royals from the Civil List, but in 2011 it was abolished altogether and replaced with the Sovereign Grant Act, designed solely to support the expenses of the working monarchy. Its inception symbolised the most significant reforms to the royal finances since the creation of the list in 1760. Rather than receiving a fixed head of state allowance from the government, the monarchy would receive an annual lump sum drawn from the Crown Estate's annual profits. Chancellor George Osborne announced that the initial share would be set at fifteen per cent, to cover the projected annual royal bill of £35 million. When Elizabeth acceded, the entire royal family was funded by the state; the monarch was exempt from tax and the queen's Civil List income was £475,000 – the equivalent of sixty per cent of the Crown Estate profits. Sixty years on, with the monarchy operating on fifteen per cent of the Crown Estate's profits and the sovereign's status as a taxpayer, the palace is better able to defend its position that the royals are good value for money.

The queen is the most widely travelled British monarch in history, having visited 116 nations over the course of her reign. She was the first British monarch to visit the Vatican, a mosque and a Hindu temple. During her 1979 trip to the Middle East – in which she became the first British monarch, first female sovereign and the world's first female head of state to visit Saudi Arabia, a strictly Muslim country – she was declared an 'honorary man'. Still, it wasn't until May 2011, aged 85, that she was finally able to visit the Republic of Ireland. The four-day state visit, designed to serve as a symbol of friendship and reconciliation, was the first by a British sovereign since the bloody struggle for Irish independence during the reign of her grandfather, George V, who last visited in 1911. The trip posed enormous security concerns, but her presence drew broad acclaim from Irish politicians. She wore emerald green, spoke a little

Gaelic and bowed before Dublin's nationalist memorial to those killed in the fight for independence. At a state banquet held at Dublin Castle she declared: 'To all those who have suffered as a consequence of our troubled past, I extend my sincere thoughts and deep sympathy. With the benefit of historical hindsight, we can all see things which we wish we had done differently or not at all.'[41] Her words received widespread praise. Progress had been made.

With William and Catherine's wedding serving as the catalyst, it was also time for progress to be made in terms of the laws to succession – which gave younger born brothers precedence over their elder sisters – and the laws forbidding monarchs from marrying Roman Catholics. In order for any reforms to be pushed through, consent was required from the other fifteen realms, and the 2011 Commonwealth summit in Australia presented the perfect opportunity to discuss the suggested amendments. Politically neutral, the queen was not able to express her opinion, but her opening remarks at the start of the summit indicated her support: 'The theme of this year is "Women as Agents of Change". It reminds us of the potential in our societies that is yet to be fully unlocked, and it encourages us to find ways to allow girls and women to play their full part.'[42] The proposed reforms were met with unanimous approval.

History was assured yet again on 6 February 2012 when Elizabeth joined her great-great-grandmother Queen Victoria in becoming one of only two British sovereigns to celebrate a diamond jubilee. Echoing her 21st birthday speech, she used the occasion to re-dedicate herself to the nation and reaffirm her commitment to the Realms and the Commonwealth. Given her advancing years, younger members of the family were dispatched on international tours to the Realms while the queen and Prince Philip conducted an extensive tour of the UK. The year also afforded the queen an opportunity to try something new. In March she invited the Duchess of Cornwall and the Duchess of Cambridge to join her on an official outing to Fortnum & Mason, a speciality food store. The reigning queen and two future queens had never conducted an engagement together. Believing the sovereign should be the main attraction, the Queen Mother would not have looked favourably upon such a collaboration, but for Elizabeth, a queen ever more relaxed in her role and not one for issuing instructions, it offered a chance to lead by example and signified her approval of the two women waiting in the wings. A week later the Duchess of Cambridge was invited to join her again as she and Prince Philip undertook an away day in Leicester. A new precedent had been set, and the queen continues to carry out occasional engagements with family members.

Central celebrations for the Diamond Jubilee took place during the first weekend in June. The entire royal family gathered on the Thames for the greatest river pageant since the reign of Charles II. Joined by the Prince of Wales and the Duchess of Cornwall, the Duke and Duchess of Cambridge and Prince Harry, the queen and the Duke of Edinburgh led the flotilla aboard *The Spirit of Chartwell*. Jubilee organisers were eager for national events to focus on the continuity of the monarchy, so it was the core family members who were to remain front and centre. Despite torrential rain, biting cold and gusty winds, over 1 million people lined the banks of the river as the 1000-boat strong flotilla set sail. Sheltered only by a limp awning, the queen stood on the upper-deck for the two-hour voyage from Putney to Tower Bridge. Mooring just beyond the Tower of London, she stood for another hour to watch the remaining procession sail past. The stamina exhibited by her and Prince Philip was astounding, but the next day news broke that Philip had been hospitalised with a bladder infection. He was not believed to be seriously ill, but given his hospitalisation for chest pains only months earlier, it reaffirmed the enormous pressures of the job for one his age. Only halfway through the weekend's celebrations, the queen would have to continue without her husband – the longest-serving consort in history, as well as the longest-lived male member of the British royal family – by her side. That night, at the conclusion of the jubilee concert staged in front of Buckingham Palace – and much to the crowd's raucous delight – Prince Charles introduced his mother saying, 'Your Majesty – Mummy …'[243] He thanked her for 'inspiring us with your selfless duty and service, and for making us proud to be British'. Events concluded the next day with a National Service of Thanksgiving at St Paul's Cathedral. Arriving to chants of 'God Save the Queen', Elizabeth cut a solitary figure as she ascended the cathedral steps and walked the imposing aisle alone. Given the duke's absence, the day ended with an appearance by six of the seven core family members on the balcony at Buckingham Palace. Their number clearly illustrated the slimmed down monarchy of the future.

Hot on the heels of 2011's royal wedding, over 1 million flag-waving members of the public flocked to the capital for each day of the Diamond Jubilee celebrations. A surge of national pride bolstered public support for the monarchy, solidified further upon the queen's surprise cameo alongside James Bond (played by Daniel Craig) during the opening ceremony of the London Olympics weeks later.

As the year drew to a close, an announcement from St James's Palace on 3 December provided the perfect finale to what could only be described as an exceptional period for the royal family – the Duchess of Cambridge was pregnant with her first child.

9

A Job For Life

In a way I didn't have an apprenticeship. My father died much too young and so it was all a very sudden kind of taking on ... I think continuity is very important. It is a job for life.

Elizabeth II, in *Elizabeth R*, 1992[44]

With three generations of heirs in waiting and European monarchs falling like dominoes, speculation over the queen's potential to abdicate mounted. In April 2013, Queen Beatrix of the Netherlands stepped down after a thirty-three year reign. In July, 79-year-old Albert II of Belgium renounced his throne, citing advancing age and health issues, and in June 2014 King Juan Carlos of Spain also announced his intention to abdicate after a reign spanning four decades. Due to the queen's own advancing years, Prince Charles has recently stepped in to represent his mother at a number of high profile engagements, most notably the Commonwealth Heads of Government meeting in Sri Lanka in November 2013. It was the first summit she had missed since 1973, but her absence was by no means an indication of her plans to step aside. Indeed, she attended the 2015 Commonwealth conference held in Malta, accompanied by Philip, Charles and Camilla. Despite being long passed pensionable age her energy remains undiminished. The queen carries out in excess of 400 engagements per year and continues to make international state visits. She is patron of over 600 charities and organisations, 400 of which she has held since 1952. She has conferred over 400,000 honours and personally presided over 610 investitures. She has given her assent to more than 3,500 Acts of Parliament and – excluding 1959 and 1963, when she was pregnant with Andrew and Edward respectively – she has attended every state opening of Parliament. From the Royal Maundy Service to Trooping the Colour, and on to the Order of the Garter service, Royal Ascot, the summer garden parties and Remembrance Day, the royal calendar is regimented and inflexible. With each occasion steeped in ceremony and tradition, the queen recognises the weight of her presence. In a speech to both Houses of Parliament commemorating her Diamond Jubilee in 2012, she rededicated herself to her country and its people, vowing to serve, 'now and in the years to come.'[45] Abdication would only be an option if Elizabeth became incapacitated.

In looking at the queen's reign, the continued existence of the Commonwealth of Nations has arguably been one of her crowning achievements. She has overseen its transition from Empire to Commonwealth. At the time of her accession the voluntary organisation numbered eight countries. Today it consists of fifty-three independent nations (encompassing 2 billion citizens), many of which chose to retain the queen as head of state. Though she has no formal power, she serves as the Commonwealth's symbolic figurehead. There are those who question the validity of the Commonwealth, citing political repression by member states and its failure to take action over alleged human rights abuses, but according to many world leaders, it endures because of the dialogue it fosters between member countries and a shared deep-rooted fondness for the queen. Upon her death it will represent a tangible lasting legacy.

In 1952, the year of Elizabeth's accession, Britain was fundamentally considered a white, Christian country at the centre of a great empire. It was an age in which men dominated politics and industry and the majority of women were housewives. Today, it is a culturally diverse nation in which multi-faith communities live side by side and women are often the primary or sole breadwinners. An unlikely feminist role model, the queen has held the highest position in the land for over six decades. There are some who look at her and see wealth, privilege and an out-dated institution, but for others she is viewed as a beacon of stability and continuity. Never changing, but rather adapting and evolving to meet the needs of the nation, she serves as a single focus for unity. In 2014, she took the top spot in a moral leadership poll, finishing well ahead of the Archbishop of Canterbury and the prime minister, a publically elected figure.

Together the queen and Prince Philip have set numerous records. In 2007, Elizabeth became the first British monarch to celebrate a Diamond Wedding Anniversary. Her husband has spent his public life walking one step behind his wife, but theirs has been a happy union and the nation has been fortunate that the queen chose a consort whose devotion to service equals her own.

It has been more than sixty years since Elizabeth pledged to serve both god and the people. As the longest serving monarch in British history, the oldest-lived British monarch and the oldest-serving monarch in the world, she has been resolute in her commitment to uphold the promises set forth in her coronation oath. But it is unlikely that the queen, now entering her tenth decade, spends much time reflecting on the achievements of her reign. She is one who has always preferred to look to the future.

With Prince Charles – Britain's longest-serving heir apparent – waiting in the wings, the preservation of the

British monarchy ultimately rests in his hands and those of his successors, but Elizabeth will leave behind the single greatest blueprint of any previous sovereign. While the monarchy remains a complex source of contention, it is Elizabeth's consistency and commitment to duty that has retained her place in the people's affections and allowed her queenship to endure well into the twenty-first century. Elected officials come and go, but under her reign, the British monarchy maintains a solid link to Britain's past. In a letter to Queen Mary in 1929 Elizabeth's mother said of her daughter, 'It almost frightens me that the people should love her so much. I suppose it is a good thing, and I hope she will be worthy of it …'[46]

Were her parents alive today they might both say she has been very worthy indeed.

Notes

1   *Elizabeth R*, p. 5

2   *Diamond Jubilee Speech to Houses of Parliament*, 20 March 2012

3   Twenty-first birthday radio address to the Commonwealth, 21 April 1947

4   *Winston and Clementine: The Personal Letters of the Churchills from Winston Churchill to his Wife*, p. 328

5   *Majesty Elizabeth II and the House of Windsor,* p. 46

6   *Daily Telegraph*, 20 April 2010, online

7   *Majesty Elizabeth II and the House of Windsor*, p. 74

8   Broadcast, outbreak of war with Germany, 3 September 1939

9   *The Queen Mother: The Official Biography*, p. 516

10   'Children's Hour' address, 13 October 1940

11   BBC recording of 1985, re-released 8 May 2015

12   Golden Wedding Anniversary speech, 20 November 1997

13   *The Little Princesses*, p. 150

14   *The Queen: The Life of Elizabeth II*, p. 133

15   Christmas address, 25 December 1952

16   *The Queen: The Life of Elizabeth II*, p. 153

17   *Philip and Elizabeth: Portrait of a Marriage*, pp. 253–4

18   *Majesty Elizabeth II and the House of Windsor*, p. 205

19   *Monarchy and the End of Empire: The House of Windsor, the British Government and the Post-war Commonwealth*, p. 99

20   *The Independent*, 4 February 2012, online

21   *The Queen: The Life of Elizabeth II*, p. 196

22   *Elizabeth II: Portrait of a Monarch*, p. 116

23 Christmas address, 25 December 2008

24 Prince Charles engagement interview, 24 February 1981

25 *The Independent*, 29 October 2009, obituary page

26 *The Sunday Times*, 20 July 1986, online

27 Christmas address, 25 December 1957

28 *The Queen, Elizabeth II and the Monarchy*, p. 538

29 *Elizabeth R,* documentary, 6 February 1992, BBC 1

30 *The Prince of Wales*, p. 489

31 The queen's speech marking the fortieth anniversary of her accession, 24 November 1992

32 Christmas address, 25 December 1992

33 *The Queen, Elizabeth II and the Monarchy*, p. 307

34 *Charles: The Private Man, the Public Role*, documentary, 29 June 1994, ITV

35 *Panorama*, 20 November 1995, BBC 1

35 Speech following the death of Diana, Princess of Wales, 5 September 1997

37 *The Queen and Di: The Untold Story*, p. 97

38 Golden Wedding Anniversary speech, 20 November 1997

39 *Queen and Country: The Fifty Year Reign of Elizabeth II*, p. 216

40 Queen's Diamond Jubilee message, 6 February 2012

41 Queen's speech at the Irish state dinner, 18 May 2011

42 Opening remarks at the 2011 Commonwealth summit, 28 October 2011

43 Diamond Jubilee concert, 4 June 2012, BBC 1

44 *Elizabeth R* documentary, 6 February 1992, BBC 1

45 Diamond Jubilee speech to Houses of Parliament, 20 March 2012

46 *The Queen Mother: The Official Biography*, p. 307

Timeline

1926	Birth of Princess Elizabeth of York on 21 April
1930	Birth of Princess Margaret of York on 21 August
1936	Edward VIII abdicates the throne
1937	Coronation of King George VI
1939	A 13-year-old Elizabeth meets 18-year-old Prince Philip The Second World War begins
1940	Princess Elizabeth's first radio address
1945	Princess Elizabeth joins the WATS VE Day on 8 May VJ Day on 15 August
1947	Elizabeth's first overseas tour Elizabeth and Philip's engagement announced on 9 July Elizabeth and Philip marry on 20 November
1948	Birth of Prince Charles on 14 November
1950	Birth of Princess Anne on 15 August
1952	Elizabeth and Philip depart for Kenya on 31 January King George VI died on 6 February and Elizabeth became queen
1953	Coronation Day on 2 June
1953-54	The queen and Prince Philip embark on a six-month tour of the Commonwealth

1955	Winston Churchill resigns as prime minister and is succeeded by Anthony Eden
1956	The Suez Crisis
1957	Harold MacMillan named prime minister
	The queen addresses the United Nations and opens the twenty-third Canadian parliament
	First televised Christmas broadcast
1960	Birth of Prince Andrew on 19 February
	Princess Margaret marries Anthony Armstrong-Jones
1963	Alec Douglas-Home replaces Harold MacMillan as prime minister
1964	Birth of Prince Edward on 10 March
	Labour prime minister Harold Wilson takes office
1969	*The Royal Family* documentary aired
	Prince Charles invested as Prince of Wales
1970	Edward Heath becomes prime minister
	The queen attends her first Commonwealth Games
1972	The queen travels to first CHOGM held outside Britain
1973	Princess Anne marries Captain Mark Phillips
1977	The queen marks her Silver Jubilee
	Birth of the queen's first grandson, Peter Phillips
1979	Lord Mountbatten is assassinated by the IRA
	Margaret Thatcher is elected the country's first female prime minister

1981	Prince Charles marries Lady Diana Spencer on 29 July
1982	Falklands War
	Birth of Prince William on 21 June
	Michael Fagan breaks into the queen's bedroom at Buckingham Palace
1984	Birth of Prince Harry on 15 September
1986	Prince Andrew marries Sarah Ferguson on 23 July
1990	Margaret Thatcher resigns and is succeeded by John Major
1991	First Gulf War
1992	*Elizabeth R* film aired
	Princess Anne and Mark Phillips divorce
	The Prince and Princess of Wales and the Duke and Duchess of York agree to separate
	Fire at Windsor Castle
	Princess Anne marries Commander Timothy Laurence
1993	Buckingham Palace State Rooms open to the public
1995	Fiftieth anniversaries of VE and VJ Day
1996	Andrew and Sarah divorce
	Charles and Diana divorce
1997	Tony Blair becomes prime minister
	Diana, Princess of Wales dies in a car crash in Paris on 31 August
	Hong Kong reverts to China after 155 years of British rule

	The queen and Prince Philip celebrate their Golden Wedding Anniversary
1999	Prince Edward marries Sophie Rhys-Jones
2000	Queen Mother celebrates her 100th birthday
2002	The queen celebrates her Golden Jubilee
	Princess Margaret and the Queen Mother both die
2005	Prince Charles marries Camilla Parker Bowles
2006	The queen celebrates her 80th birthday
2007	Tony Blair resigns
	The queen and Prince Philip celebrate their Diamond Wedding Anniversary
2010	The queen becomes a great-grandmother upon the birth of Savannah Phillips
	David Cameron becomes prime minister
2011	Prince William marries Catherine Middleton
	Prince Philip celebrates his 90th birthday
	The queen makes her first state visit to the Republic of Ireland
2012	The queen celebrates her Diamond Jubilee
	London hosts the 2012 Summer Olympics
2013	Birth of Prince George of Cambridge on 22 July
2014	Scottish voters reject proposal by the Scottish National Party to leave the UK
2015	The queen becomes the oldest serving monarch in the world

Birth of Princess Charlotte of Cambridge on 2 May

The Conservative Party, led by David Cameron, wins the General Election

Seventieth anniversaries of VE and VJ Day

The queen becomes the longest-serving monarch in British history on 9 September

2016	The queen celebrates her 90th birthday

Further Reading

Bedell Smith, Sally, *Elizabeth the Queen: The Woman Behind the Throne* (Penguin, 2012)

Brandreth, Gyles, *Philip and Elizabeth: Portrait of a Royal Marriage* (W.W. Norton & Company, 2006)

Crawford, Marion, *The Little Princesses* (Cassell & Co. Ltd, 1950)

Eade, Philip, *Young Prince Philip* (Harper Press, 2012)

Hardman, Robert, *Her Majesty Queen Elizabeth II and Her Court* (Pegasus Books LLC, 2012)

Kelly, Angela, *Dressing the Queen: The Jubilee Wardrobe* (The Royal Collection Trust, 2012)

Lacey, Robert, *Majesty Elizabeth II and the House of Windsor* (Harcourt Brace Jovanovich, 1977)

Longford, Elizabeth, *The Queen* (Alfred A. Knopf, Inc., 1983)

Marr, Andrew, *The Real Elizabeth* (Griffin, Reprint Edition 2013)

Marr, Andrew, *The Diamond Queen* (Pan, 2012)

Pimlott, Ben, *The Queen* (Harper Press, 1996)

Rhodes, Margaret, *The Final Curtsey: A Royal Memoir by the Queen's Cousin* (Birlinn, 2012)

Shawcross, William, *The Queen Mother: The Official Biography* (Macmillan, 2009)

Starkey, David, *A History of England through the Monarchy* (Harper Press, Reprint Edition 2011)

Wheeler-Bennett, John, *King George VI: His Life and Reign* (Macmillan, 1958)

Weblinks

BBC documentary, 'The Diamond Queen', Ep. 1
– www.youtube.com/watch?v=HgweMOYZRZs
BBC documentary, 'The Diamond Queen', Ep. 2
– www.youtube.com/watch?v=yMBZo1MHqCY
BBC documentary, 'The Diamond Queen', Ep. 3
– www.youtube.com/watch?v=3jv_PFgfpLI
British Pathé (archival footage) – www.britishpathe.com/
workspaces/BritishPathe/coronation
Documentary, *Elizabeth R* (1992) – www.youtube.com/
watch?v=snSv_3xYUho
Historic Royal Palaces – www.hrp.org.uk
Majesty Magazine – www.majestymagazine.com
Official website of the British monarchy
– www.royal.gov.uk
Official website for the Prince of Wales
– www.princeofwales.gov.uk
Official website for the Duke and Duchess of Cambridge
– www.dukeandduchessofcambridge.org
Queen recounts VE Day 1945 – www.youtube.com/
watch?v=kGfpcOmYefo
Royal Collection Trust – www.royalcollection.org.uk
Royal Yacht Britannia – www.royalyachtbritannia.co.uk
Sandringham Estate – www.sandringhamestate.co.uk
Westminster Abbey – www.westminster-abbey.org/home

Giuseppe Verdi Henry V **Brunel** Pope John Paul II **Jane Austen** Sigmund Freud **Abraham Lincoln** Robert the Bruce **Charles Darwin** Buddha **Elizabeth I** Horatio Nelson **Wellington** Hannibal & Scipio **Jesus** Joan of Arc **Anne Frank** Alfred the Great **King Arthur** Henry Ford **Nelson Mandela** Edward Jenner **Napoleon Bonaparte** Isaac Newton **Albert Einstein** John Lennon **Elizabeth II**